8.27
9.35

Basic Decimals

by Jerome D. Kaplan, Ed.D.

Editor: Caleb E. Crowell

Illustrator: Michael McDermott

EDUCATIONAL DESIGN, INC.
EDI 334

ISBN# 0-87694-398-9   EDI 334

Table of Contents

Introduction

To the Student

Decimals are everywhere these days. You can't read a price tag or write an amount of dollars and cents without using them. You also find decimals on the readouts of many electronic devices such as timers (for example, 6.4 seconds) and digital thermometers (56.3 degrees). You find them on computer screens and on calculators. It is because of these last two that everybody needs to study decimals even more than before. You can't understand the modern world unless you understand decimals.

This book, **Basic Decimals**, will make learning decimals easy. It takes you from the beginning of decimals, and slowly and carefully introduces you to all the concepts and skills that you need. As you move through the book from one chapter to the next, and from one lesson to the next, you will learn how to work with decimals one step at a time. You will master one skill, then go on to the next one—which is based on the one you just learned. You will not be making big jumps or disconnected jumps. Everything you read and do will be clear to you.

Each lesson deals with a single skill. It starts with a real-life example of how the skill is used. It then gives you one or two simple rules plus several more examples to illustrate how to use the rules are used. Finally, there is an exercise section for you to practice the skill. Some of the special things about this book are in the exercise section. There are two parts: **Exercises with Hints** and **Exercises on Your Own.** The questions of the first part come with hints that guide you in solving the problems. This helps you get ready to do the problems _without_ hints in the second section. As in the rest of the lesson, everything is done in steps, slowly and carefully. You will also find that the word problems at the end of the exercises are good examples of where and how decimals are used.

Good luck with **Basic Decimals.**

1. Tenths, Hundredths, and Thousandths

1.1 Decimals for Tenths

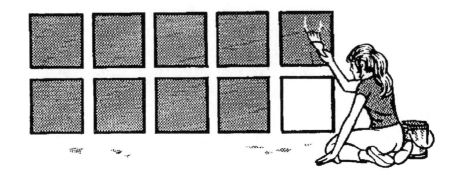

Hana finished 9 of the 10 panels she was painting.

What is the decimal number that shows how much she finished?

She painted 9 of 10 equal parts.

The fraction that shows how much she finished is $\frac{9}{10}$.

The decimal number that shows the same amount is written 0.9.

$$\frac{9}{10} = 0.9$$

We read the decimal in the same way as we read the fraction.

We say "9 tenths."

Sometimes we read it another way. We say, "Point 9."

Notice that we first write a 0 before the decimal point, but don't say it.

HOW TO *recognize and say decimals for tenths:*

> *1.* Find the decimal point.
> *2.* The place to the right of the decimal point shows tenths:
>   0. [tenths]
> *3.* For example: 0.4 Say "4 tenths."

EXAMPLE 1

What fraction does 0.8 show?

8 is to the right of the decimal point.

The number 0.8 shows 8 of 10 equal parts, or 8 tenths.

$$0.8 = \frac{8}{10}$$

EXAMPLE 2

What decimal stands for $\frac{7}{10}$?

$\frac{7}{10}$ stands for 7 of 10 equal parts.

Write 7 to the right of the decimal point.

$$\frac{7}{10} = 0.7$$

Don't forget the 0 before the decimal point.

EXAMPLE 3

How do you say 0.2?

2 is in the tenths place.

Say "2 tenths."

(You can also say "Point 2.")

Exercises with Hints

Write a decimal for each.
(Hint: 4 of 10 means 4 tenths. Remember the 0 before the decimal point.)

1. 4 of 10   _____

2. 2 of 10   _____

3. 8 of 10   _____

Write the fraction for each decimal.
(Hint: The number to the right of the decimal point is in the tenths place.)

4. 0.1   _____

5. 0.9   _____

6. 0.3   _____

Write the decimal for each fraction.

(Hint: $\frac{3}{10}$ means 3 of 10 equal parts.)

7. $\frac{3}{10}$ _____

8. $\frac{8}{10}$ _____

9. $\frac{2}{10}$ _____

Write the decimal for each.
(Hint: For tenths, there is one place to the right of the decimal point.)

10. 6 tenths _____

11. 5 tenths _____

12. 4 tenths _____

Solve.

13. Angela placed 10 straws on the table. Her friends used 7 of them. Write the decimal for the straws that were used. *(Hint: Write the decimal for 7 of 10.)*

_____

14. Francisco saw a sign that read:

**0.9 mile to
Yellowstone National Park.**

Write this decimal as a fraction. *(Hint: The number to the right of the decimal point is in the tenths place.)*

_____

15. Carla drank $\frac{4}{10}$ liter of water. Write this fraction as a decimal: *(Hint: 4 out of 10 means 4 of 10 equal parts.)*

_____

Exercises on Your Own _____

Write the decimal for each fraction.

1. $\frac{7}{10}$ _____

2. $\frac{3}{10}$ _____

3. $\frac{9}{10}$ _____

Write the fraction for each decimal.

4. 0.1 _____

5. 0.8 _____

6. 0.2 _____

Write the decimal for each.

7. 7 tenths _____

8. 4 tenths _____

9. 5 tenths _____

Write a decimal for each.

10. 3 of 10 _____

11. 1 of 10 _____

12. 7 of 10 _____

Solve.

13. Carla sold 8 of the 10 ties she had. Write a decimal to show the part she sold.

_____

14. Spike drank 2 of the 10 cans of soda in the refrigerator. Write a decimal to show what part of the sodas he drank.

_____

15. Gloria drank 0.6 liters of soda. Write this decimal as a fraction.

_____

1.2 Comparing and Ordering Decimals in Tenths

George cut two boards for a book case.

One board is 0.7 meters long, and the other

board is 0.5 meters long. Which board is longer?

To compare two decimals, use a number line:

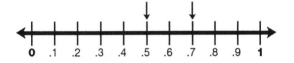

Compare 0.7 and 0.5 on a number line in the same way you compare whole numbers:

0.7 is to the right of 0.5, so 0.7 is greater than 0.5.

The board that is 0.7 meters is longer than the board that is 0.5 meters.

- -

The symbols **>** and **<** are often used to compare numbers.

The symbol **>** means **"is greater than."**

0.7 > 0.5   (That is, 0.7 **is greater than** 0.5)

The symbol **<** means **"is less than."**

0.5 < 0.7   (That is, 0.5 **is less than** 0.7)

REMEMBER:

Here's a way to remember the difference between the symbols **>** and **<**.

The symbol **>** has the greater (larger) end first. It means **"is greater than."**

The symbol **<** has the lesser (smaller) end first. It means **"is less than."**

HOW TO *compare and order decimals in tenths:*

---

1. Draw a number line.
2. Locate the numbers on the line.
3. A number to the right of another number is the greater number.
4. For more than two numbers, follow the order of the numbers on the number line.

EXAMPLE 1

Compare 0.6 and 0.3.

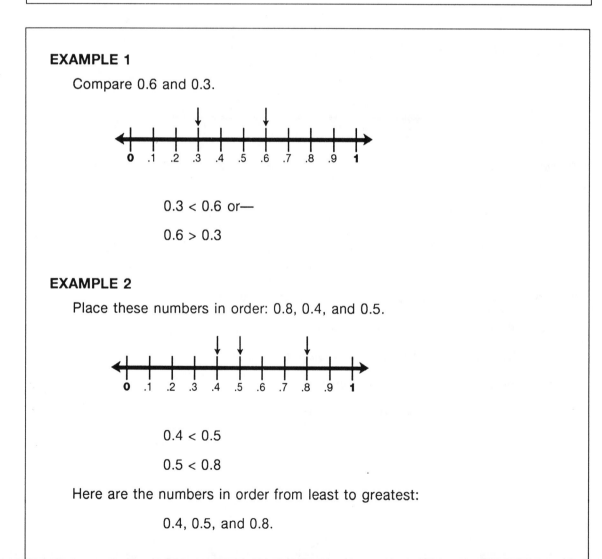

0.3 < 0.6 or—

0.6 > 0.3

EXAMPLE 2

Place these numbers in order: 0.8, 0.4, and 0.5.

0.4 < 0.5

0.5 < 0.8

Here are the numbers in order from least to greatest:

0.4, 0.5, and 0.8.

Exercises with Hints

Locate each number on the number line by placing the letter on the line.
(Hint: Match the number with its position on the number line.)

1. A = 0.6

2. B = 0.2

3. C = 0.9

4. D = 0.1

Compare these numbers. Write the greater number in the blanks.
(Hint: Use the number line to help you. Remember, on the number line, the number to the right is the greater number.)

5. 0.2 and 0.4 _____

6. 0.7 and 0.6 _____

7. 0.9 and 0.8 _____

Use a number line to place these numbers in order from least to greatest.
(Hint: The number farthest to the right on the number line is the greatest number.)

8. 0.3, 0.1, 0.7 _____

9. 0.6, 0.2, 0.5 _____

10. 0.4, 0.9, 0.1 _____

Solve.

11. Grace works as a chemist. She weighed three tablets very carefully. The yellow tablet weighed 0.7 grams, the blue tablet weighed 0.6 grams, and the green tablet weighed 0.9 grams.

    a. Which tablet is the heaviest?

    _____

    (Hint: Write the decimals without the decimal points and compare.)

    b. Which tablet weighs the least?

    _____

Exercises on Your Own

Complete these with **<** or **>**.

1. 0.4 ___ 0.3

2. 0.8 ___ 0.9

3. 0.5 ___ 0.3

4. 0.6 ___ 0.5

5. 0.6 ___ 0.4

6. 0.1 ___ 0.2

Place each set of decimals in order from the least to the greatest.

7. 0.2, 0.5, 0.1 _____

8. 0.6, 0.5, 0.3 _____

9. 0.2, 0.8, 0.1 _____

10. 0.3, 0.5, 0.2, 0.8 _____

11. 0.2, 0.7, 0.5, 0.3 _____

12. Karl bought 0.4 kilograms of cheese, 0.6 kilograms of turkey, and 0.3 kilograms of salami.
Did he buy—

   a. more salami or turkey? _____

   b. more turkey or cheese? _____

13. Alva took 0.5 hour to finish her report. Dana took 0.7 hour, and John took 0.6 hour.

   a. Who took the longest to finish the report? _____

   b. Who took the least amount of time? _____

1.3 Decimals For Hundredths

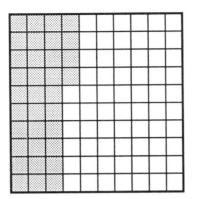

Marge is painting a pattern she is making. There are 100 small squares in the grid. She has to paint 34 of them.

What is the decimal number that shows what she has painted?

She painted 34 of 100 equal parts.
The fraction that shows how much she painted is $\frac{34}{100}$.

The <u>decimal number</u> that shows the same amount is 0.34.

$$\frac{34}{100} = 0.34$$

We read the decimal in the same way that we read the fraction.

We say "34 hundredths."

Or we say "Point 34."

Notice that we still write a 0 before the decimal point.

HOW TO *recognize and say decimals in hundredths:*

> **1.** Find the decimal point.
>
> **2.** The <u>second</u> place to the right of the decimal point shows <u>hundredths</u>.
>
> | | *0* | *. tenths* | *hundredths* |
> |---|---|---|---|
> | | 0 | .   4 | 6 |
>
> **3.** In this example, there are 4 tenths and 6 hundredths.
> Since 4 tenths = 40 hundredths, there are 46 hundredths.
> Say "46 hundredths."

EXAMPLE 1

What fraction does 0.17 show?

17 occupies two places to the right of the decimal point.

So the decimal stands for 17 hundredths:

$$0.17 = \frac{17}{100}$$

EXAMPLE 2

What decimal stands for $\frac{84}{100}$?

$\frac{84}{100}$ stands for 84 out of 100 equal parts.

Write 84 to the right of the decimal point.

$$\frac{84}{100} = 0.84$$

EXAMPLE 3

How do you say 0.67?

There are two places to the right of the decimal point, so the decimal stands for hundredths.

Say "67 hundredths."

(Or say "Point 67.")

EXAMPLE 4

What fraction does 0.04 stand for?

There are two places, 0 and 4, to the right of the decimal point.

So the decimal stands for 4 hundredths:

$$0.04 = \frac{4}{100}$$

This is tricky, and catches a lot of people. Be sure you understand it before you go on!

EXAMPLE 5

What decimal stands for $\frac{6}{100}$? (It is NOT 0.6!)

Remember, in writing hundredths there are two places to the right of the decimal point.

$$\frac{6}{100} = 0.06$$

This is tricky, just like Example 4 is. Be sure you understand both this example and Example 4 before you go on!

Exercises with Hints

Write a decimal for each.
(Hint: 39 of 100 means 39 hundredths. Look at Example 2.)

1. 39 of 100 _____

2. 81 of 100 _____

3. 50 of 100 _____

Write the fraction for each decimal.
(Hint: Two places to the right of the decimal point means that the decimal stands for hundredths. Look at Example 1.)

4. 0.73 _____

5. 0.48 _____

6. 0.07 _____
   (Hint: Look at Example 4.)

Write the decimal for each fraction.
(Hint: $\frac{43}{100}$ means 43 of 100 equal parts. Look at Example 2.)

7. $\frac{43}{100}$ _____

8. $\frac{74}{100}$ _____

9. $\frac{9}{100}$ _____
   (Hint: Look at Example 5.)

Write the decimal for each.
(Hint: For hundredths, place the number so that there are two places to the right of the decimal point. Look at Example 2.)

10. 82 hundredths _____

11. 65 hundredths _____

12. 7 hundredths _____
   (Hint: Look at Example 5.)

Solve.

13. Joan found that 6 of 100 chips were defective. Write the decimal for the part of the total number of chips that were defective.
   (Hint: Write the decimal for 6 of 100.)

   _____

14. Ricardo said that he lost by 9 hundredths of a second. Write this time as a decimal.
   (Hint: "Hundredths" means two decimal places.)

   _____

Exercises on Your Own

Write the decimal for each fraction.

1. $\frac{48}{100}$ _____

2. $\frac{30}{100}$ _____

3. $\frac{1}{100}$ _____

Write the fraction for each decimal.

4. 0.81 _____

5. 0.25 _____

6. 0.06 _____
(Hint: Look at Example 4)

Write the decimal for each.

7. 8 hundredths _____

8. 17 hundredths _____

9. 69 hundredths _____

Write a decimal for each.

10. 43 of 100 _____

11. 3 of 100 _____

12. 82 of 100 _____

Solve.

11. Mike's time for the 100-meter distance was $\frac{47}{100}$ seconds faster than his time yesterday. Write this fraction as a decimal.

_____

12. It rained 6 out of 100 days. Write a decimal for the fraction of days that it rained.

_____

13. Angela shot the basket that won the game with 0.67 seconds left. Write the fraction that is the same as this decimal number.

_____

1.4 Comparing and Ordering Decimals in Hundredths

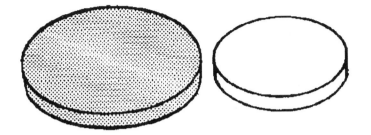

Dennis measures two disks. The diameter of the gray one is 0.16 meters, and the diameter of the white one is 0.12 meters. Which one is wider?

Compare decimals the same way that you compare whole numbers.

To compare 0.16 and 0.12, compare 16 and 12:

Since 16 >12, then 0.16 > 0.12.

The gray disk is wider than the white disk.

HOW TO *compare and order decimals in hundredths:*

---

1. Write the decimals without the decimal point—as whole numbers.

2. Compare the whole numbers.

EXAMPLE 1

Compare 0.47 and 0.61.

Write the numbers as 47 and 61.

Since 47 < 61, then 0.47 < 0.61. (Or, 0.61 > 0.47)

EXAMPLE 2

Compare 0.07 and 0.70.

Write the numbers as 7 and 70. (Notice that .07 becomes just plain 7.)

Since 7 < 70, then 0.07 < 0.70.

EXAMPLE 3

Place these numbers in order from least to greatest:

0.40, 0.48, and 0.04.

Write the numbers without the decimal points:

40, 48, and 4.

The order of these numbers from least to greatest is 4, 40, and 48.
So the order of the decimal numbers is 0.04, 0.40, and 0.48.

Exercises with Hints

Write these numbers without the decimal points.
(Hint: Write the numbers as whole numbers.)

1. 0.89 _____

2. 0.40 _____

3. 0.03 _____

4. 0.16 _____

Compare these numbers. Which is greater in each pair?
(Hint: First write the numbers as whole numbers, then compare.)

5. 0.94 and 0.91 _____

6. 0.22 and 0.03 _____

7. 0.60 and 0.37 _____

Place these numbers in order from least to greatest.
(Hint: Write the numbers as whole numbers first.)

8. 0.21, 0.19, and 0.02 _____

9. 0.55, 0.50, and 0.64 _____

Solve.

10. The weather report said that 0.45 inch of rain fell on Tuesday and that 0.38 inch fell on Wednesday. On which day was there more rain?
(Hint: Write the numbers without the decimals points and compare.)

_____

Exercises on Your Own _____

Which number is greater?

1. 0.68 or 0.86 _____

2. 0.31 or 0.37 _____

3. 0.49 or 0.40 _____

4. 0.19 or 0.90 _____

5. 0.02 or 0.20 _____

6. 0.55 or 0.05 _____

Place these numbers in order from least to greatest.

7. 0.11, 0.21, and 0.55 _____

8. 0.06, 0.60, and 0.66 _____

9. 0.85, 0.89, and 0.08 _____

10. 0.04, 0.07, and 0.05 _____

11. 0.37, 0.32, 0.39, and 0.03 _____

Solve.

12. Selene measured two wires. One was 0.47 inch, the other was 0.74 inch. Which was longer?

_____

13. Flora measured the height of a bookcase. The right side was 0.87 meters high. The left side measured 0.93 meters high. On which side was the bookcase higher?

_____

1.5 Writing Cents and Decimals

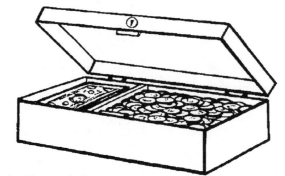

Khalil has 45 pennies in his cash box.

What part of a dollar is this?

Write your answer as a fraction. Then write it as a decimal.

Each penny or cent is 1 of 100 parts of a dollar.

45 pennies or cents is 45 of 100 parts of a dollar.

We can write 45 of 100 parts as a fraction: $\frac{45}{100}$.

We can also write 45 cents as a decimal—0.45 of a dollar.

The short way to write 0.45 of a dollar is $.45.

The symbol $ is called the <u>dollar sign</u>, and means that we are writing amounts of money.

Cents are hundredths of a dollar. If you can write hundredths in decimal form, you can write cents.

HOW TO *write cents as decimals:*

1. If the number of cents <u>has</u> two digits—
   - Write a decimal point in front of the two digits.
   - Then write the dollar sign in front of the decimal point.
     45 cents is $.45

2. If the number of cents <u>has</u> one digit—
   - First write a <u>zero</u> in front of the digit and write a decimal point in front of the zero.
   - Then write the dollar sign in front of the decimal point.
     3 cents is $.03

EXAMPLE 1

Write 82 cents as a decimal.

82 has two digits, so we write 82 cents as $.82

EXAMPLE 2

Write 7 cents as a decimal.

7 has one digit, so we write 7 cents as $.07

Exercises with Hints

Write these amounts as fractions of a dollar.
(Hint: 28 cents means 28 parts of 100.)

1. 28 cents   _____

2. 92 cents   _____

3. 6 cents   _____

Write these amounts in decimal form without the dollar sign.
(Hint: 91 cents means 91 parts of 100, or 91 hundredths.)

4. 91 cents   _____

5. 2 cents   _____

6. 55 cents   _____

Write these as money amounts in decimal form with the dollar sign.
(Hint: Use the rules listed in the lesson.)

7. 58 cents   _____

8. 70 cents   _____

9. 5 cents *(Be careful!)*   _____

10. 16 cents   _____

Write the value of these coins in decimal form with the dollar sign.
(Hint: How many cents is a nickel worth? A dime? A quarter?)

11. 1 nickel   _____

12. 1 dime   _____

13. 1 quarter   _____

Solve.

14. Doris paid $.80 for a newspaper. How many cents did she pay?
(Hint: Remove the decimal point and the dollar sign.)

_____

15. Roland spent a quarter to make a telephone. Write the value of this coin in decimal form with a dollar sign.
(Hint: How many cents is a quarter worth?)

_____

Exercises on Your Own

Write these amounts as fractions of a dollar.

1. 82 cents   _____

2. 40 cents   _____

3. 9 cents   _____

Write these amounts in decimal form without the dollar sign.

4. 14 cents   _____

5. 70 cents   _____

6. 7 cents   _____

Write these as money amounts in decimal form with the dollar sign.

7. 50 cents   _____

8. 27 cents   _____

9. 6 cents   _____

10. 35 cents   _____

Write the value of these coins in decimal form with the dollar sign.

11. a penny   _____

12. 2 nickels   _____

13. 2 dimes   _____

14. 2 quarters   _____

Solve.

15. Willis paid for a snack with 2 quarters and a dime. Add in your head to find the amount the snack cost. Write the answer in decimal form with the dollar sign.

_____

16. Rosa received a quarter and a dime as change at the super market. Add in your head to find the total amount of the change. Write the answer in decimal form with the dollar sign.

_____

1.6 Decimals For Thousands

There are 1000 students taking Adult Education courses at night at West High School. 376 of these students are over 40 years old.

Write a decimal to show the part of all the students that are over 40.

376 of 1000 students are over 40.

The fraction that shows the number of students over 40 is $\frac{376}{1000}$.

The decimal number that shows $\frac{376}{1000}$ is 0.376

$$\frac{376}{1000} = 0.376$$

We read the decimal in the same way as we read the fraction.

We say "376 thousandths." (Or we say "Point 376.")

HOW TO *recognize and say decimals for thousandths:*

1. Find the decimal point.

2. The third place to the right of the decimal point shows thousandths.

0	*. tenths*	*hundredths*	*thousandths*
0 .	3	7	6

3. In this example, there are 376 thousandths.

376 thousandths = 3 tenths, 7 hundredths, 6 thousandths

Say "376 thousandths." (Or "Point 376.")

EXAMPLE 1

What fraction does 0.235 show?

235 takes up three places to the right of the decimal point.

So the decimal stands for 235 thousandths:

$$0.235 = \frac{235}{1000}$$

EXAMPLE 2

What decimal stands for $\frac{603}{1000}$?

$\frac{603}{1000}$ stands for 603 out of 1000 equal parts.

Write 603 to the right of the decimal point.

$$\frac{603}{1000} = 0.603$$

EXAMPLE 3

How do you say 0.491?

Since there are three places to the right of the decimal point, the decimal stands for thousandths.

Say "491 thousandths."

EXAMPLE 4

What fraction does 0.038 stand for?

There are three places —0, 3, and 8—to the right of the decimal point.

So the decimal stands for 38 thousandths:

$$0.038 = \frac{38}{1000}$$

EXAMPLE 5

What fraction does 0.005 stand for?

There are three places—0, 0, and 5—to the right of the decimal point.

So the decimal stands for 5 thousandths.

$$0.005 = \frac{5}{1000}$$

Exercises with Hints

Write a decimal for each.
(Hint: 749 of 1000 means 749 thousandths. See Example 2.)

1. 749 of 1000 _____

2. 407 of 1000 _____

3. 18 of 1000 _____
(Hint: See Example 4.)

4. 6 of 10 *(Hint: Careful! The question asks for 6 of 10, not for 6 of 1000. You learned this in* Lesson 1.1.*)*

_____

5. 8 of 100 *(Hint: Careful! The question asks for 8 of 100, not for 8 of 1000. You learned this in* Lesson 1.3, *too.)*

_____

Write the fraction for each decimal.
(Hint: 3 places to the right of decimal point mean that the decimal stands for thousandths. See Example 1. But be careful of exercises with 2 places or 1 place to the right of the decimal point.)

6. 0.921 _____

7. 0.307 _____

8. 0.044 _____

9. 0.28 _____
(Hint: Is this thousandths?)

10. 0.08 *(Hint: Careful! The question asks for 0.08, not for 0.008. You learned this in* Lesson 1.3.*)*

_____

11. 0.1 *(Hint: See* Lesson 1.1.*)*

_____

Write the decimal for each fraction.
(Hint: $\frac{677}{1000}$ *means 677 of 1000 equal parts. See Example 2.)*

12. $\frac{402}{1000}$ _____

13. $\frac{9}{1000}$ _____
(Hint: See Example 5.)

Write the decimal for each.
(Hint: For thousandths, place the number so that there are 3 places to the right of the decimal point. See Example 2.)

14. 877 thousandths _____

15. 41 thousandths _____
(Hint: See Example 4.)

16. 4 thousandths _____
(Hint: See Example 5.)

Solve.

17. In a recent survey, 354 motorists out of 1000 said that they pay over $2 in highway tolls every day. Write a decimal to show 354 of 1000. *(Hint: 354 out of 1000 means 354 thousandths.)*

_____

18. Of the last 1000 foul shots, our team made 701. Write a decimal for 701 out of 1000. *(Hint: 701 out of 1000 means 701 thousandths.)*

_____

Exercises on Your Own

Write the decimal for each fraction.

1. $\dfrac{135}{1000}$ _____

2. $\dfrac{914}{1000}$ _____

3. $\dfrac{306}{1000}$ _____

4. $\dfrac{17}{1000}$ _____

5. $\dfrac{45}{100}$ _____

6. $\dfrac{7}{10}$ _____

7. $\dfrac{9}{100}$ _____

8. $\dfrac{40}{1000}$ _____

Write the fraction for each decimal.

9. 0.874 _____

10. 0.109 _____

11. 0.045 _____

12. 0.040 _____

13. 0.9 _____

14. 0.67 _____

15. 0.1 _____

16. 0.04 _____

Write a decimal for each.

17. 105 thousandths _____

18. 850 thousandths _____

19. 75 thousandths _____

20. 23 hundredths _____

21. 7 hundredths _____

22. 3 tenths _____

Write a decimal for each.

23. 756 of 1000 _____

24. 401 of 1000 _____

25. 38 of 1000 _____

26. 14 of 100 _____

27. 3 of 10 _____

28. 80 of 1000 _____

Solve.

29. Alma has to read a book 1000 pages long. She already has read 278 pages. Write a decimal to show 278 of 1000.

_____

30. At the pencil factory, it is estimated that only 3 of every 1000 pencils are defective. Write a decimal for 3 of 1000.

_____

31. Flora said that the defective rate for new calculators is less than 0.001. Write this decimal as a fraction.

_____

32. Steve conducted a survey of how many people recycle their newspapers. He asked 1000 people and found that 256 out of 1000 recycle newspapers. Write this as a fraction and then as a decimal.

Fraction: _____ Decimal: _____

1.7 Comparing and Ordering Decimals In Thousandths

Brian measured a steel pipe three different times.

He got these three lengths:

0.625 meters, 0.629 meters, and 0.622 meters.

Place these three numbers in order from least to greatest.

Compare the three decimals just as you would whole numbers.

To compare 0.625, 0.629, and 0.622, compare 625, 629, and 622.

Since 625 < 629 and 622 < 625, the order of the three whole numbers is:

622, 625, and 629.

The order of the three decimal numbers is:

0.622, 0.625, and 0.629.

HOW TO *compare and order decimals in thousandths:*

> **1.** Write the decimals without the decimal point—as whole numbers.
>
> **2.** Compare or order the whole numbers.

EXAMPLE 1

Compare 0.693 and 0.301

Write the whole numbers as 693 and 301

Since 301 < 693, then 0.301 < 0.693

EXAMPLE 2

Compare 0.045 and 0.429

Write the numbers as 45 and 429

Since 45 < 429, then 0.045 < 0.429

EXAMPLE 3

Order these numbers from least to greatest: 0.903, 0.917, 0.094

Write the numbers as whole numbers: 903, 917, 94

The order of the whole numbers is 94, 903, and 917

So the order of the decimal numbers is 0.094, 0.903, and 0.917

Exercises with Hints

Write these numbers as whole numbers. *(Hint: Write the numbers without decimal points.)*

1. 0.428 _____

2. 0.902 _____

3. 0.018 _____

4. 0.005 _____

Compare these numbers:
(Hint: See Examples 1 and 2.)

5. 0.271 and 0.673 _____

6. 0.502 and 0.511 _____

7. 0.029 and 0.026 _____

Place these numbers in order from least to greatest. *(Hint: See Example 3)*

8. 0.215, 0.271, and 0.401 _____

9. 0.002, 0.040, and 0.043 _____

10. 0.710, 0.701, and 0.715 _____

11. A grounds crew measured a football field three times. Here are the three measurements:

0.357 kilometers

0.347 kilometers

0.352 kilometers

a. Which measurement is the shortest? _____

b. Which measurement is the longest? _____
(Hint: First write the numbers without decimal points.)

28

Exercises on Your Own

Which number is greater?

1. 0.934 or 0.834 _____

2. 0.227 or 0.272 _____

3. 0.091 or 0.913 _____

4. 0.124 or 0.122 _____

5. 0.026 or 0.021 _____

6. 0.518 or 0.513 _____

Place these numbers in order from least to greatest.

7. 0.125, 0.117, and 0.711 _____

8. 0.042, 0.024, and 0 _____

9. 0.306, 0.308, 0.038 _____

10. 0.691, 0.961, and 0.169 _____

Solve.

11. Melanie came in second in each of the three 100-meter dashes she ran. She was second by 0.024 seconds, by 0.028 seconds, and by 0.017 seconds. In which race did she come closest to winning?

_____

1.8 Review

Write the decimal for each fraction.

1. $\frac{2}{10}$ _____

2. $\frac{7}{10}$ _____

3. $\frac{8}{10}$ _____

Write the fraction for each decimal.

4. 0.9 _____

5. 0.3 _____

6. 0.1 _____

Write the decimal for each.

7. 5 tenths _____

8. 8 tenths _____

9. 2 tenths _____

Write a decimal for each.

10. 4 of 10 _____

11. 9 of 10 _____

12. 2 of 10 _____

Complete these with < or >.

13. 0.6 ____ 0.7

14. 0.3 ____ 0.2

Place each set of decimals in order from the least to the greatest.

15. 0.4, 0.3, 0.7 ____ ____ ____

16. 0.2, 0.8, 0.5 ____ ____ ____

Write the decimal for each fraction.

17. $\frac{78}{100}$ _____

18. $\frac{7}{100}$ _____

Write the fraction for each decimal.

19. 0.76 _____

20. 0.08 _____

Write the decimal for each.

21. 49 hundredths _____

22. 3 hundredths _____

Write a decimal for each.

23. 18 of 100 _____

24. 4 of 100 _____

Which number is greater?

25. 0.34 or 0.43 _____

26. 0.87 or 0.82 _____

Place these numbers in order from least to greatest.

27. 0.55, 0.52, and 0.56 _____

28. 0.04, 0.40, and 0.44 _____

Write these as money amounts in decimal form with the dollar sign.

29. 43 cents _____

30. 87 cents _____

31. 9 cents _____

Write the value of these coins in decimal form with the dollar sign.

32. 3 pennies _____

33. 3 nickels _____

34. 3 dimes _____

35. 3 quarters _____

Write the decimal for each fraction.

36. $\dfrac{387}{1000}$ _____

37. $\dfrac{13}{1000}$ _____

38. $\dfrac{700}{1000}$ _____

Write the fraction for each decimal.

39. 0.206 _____

40. 0.071 _____

Write a decimal for each.

41. 984 thousandths _____

42. 38 thousandths _____

Write a decimal for each.

43. 14 of 1000 _____

44. 983 of 1000 _____

Which number is greater?

45. 0.276 or 0.274 _____

46. 0.072 or 0.075 _____

47. 0.998 or 0.967 _____

Place these numbers in order from least to greatest.

48. 0.336, 0.328, and 0.391 _____

49. 0.016, 0.003, and 0.256 _____

50. 0.228, 0.518, 0.553 _____

Solve.

51. Smith moved 3 out of 10 cartons into the warehouse before lunch. Write a decimal to show the part of the total she moved.

_____

52. Bruce's instruction manual says that he should spend 0.6 hour each day working at a computer. Write this decimal as a fraction.

_____

53. Nora divided her savings into three parts. She spent 0.3 of the money, invested 0.5 of the money, and gave 0.2 of the money to her daughter.

a. What did she do with the greatest part?

_____

b. What did she do with the smallest part?

_____

54. Meli told her group that the computer found their productivity this week was only 0.78 of their productivity last week. Write this decimal as a fraction.

_____

55. Carl read that $\frac{27}{100}$ of the people in his town vote. Write this fraction as a decimal.

_____

56. Barbara weighed two containers. The one with the salad weighed 0.45 pound. The container with fruit weighed 0.54 pound. Which weighed more, the salad or the fruit?

_____

57. Charlie paid for a highway toll with a quarter, a dime, and 2 nickels. How much did the toll cost? Write the answer in decimal form with the dollar sign.

_____

58. Charlene needs $1000 as a down payment for a car. She has $487 now. Write 487 of 1000 as a decimal.

_____

59. Marla got 1000 hits in her baseball league after three years. Nine of the hits were home runs. Write 9 of 1000 as a decimal.

_____

60. These were the measurements of the heads of three monarch butterflies in Bart's collection: 1) 0.576 centimeters; 2) 0.567 centimeters; and 3) 0.559 centimeters.

a. Which butterfly has the biggest head?

_____

b. Which butterfly has the smallest head?

_____

2. *Mixed Decimals*

2.1 *Equivalent Decimals*

Charlie looked at the number on the side of a bottle.

The label read "0.4 liters."

Write this number as a decimal in hundredths.

$$0.4 = \frac{4}{10}$$

Multiply the numerator and denominator of $\frac{4}{10}$ by 10:

$$\frac{4}{10} = \frac{4 \times \mathbf{10}}{10 \times \mathbf{10}} = \frac{40}{100}$$

Change $\frac{40}{100}$ to a decimal:

$$\frac{40}{100} = 0.40$$

So, 0.4 = 0.40.

0.4 and 0.40 are called <u>equivalent</u> decimals.

There's an even easier way to change a decimal in tenths to hundredths. Just add a zero in the second place after the decimal point.

HOW TO *change tenths to hundredths:*

> **To change a decimal from tenths to hundredths, add a zero in the second place after the decimal point.**

EXAMPLE 1

Change 0.7 to hundredths.

Add a zero in the second place after the decimal point:

$$0.7 = 0.70$$

HOW TO change hundredths to thousandths:

To change a decimal from hundredths to thousandths, add a zero in the third place after the decimal point.

EXAMPLE 2

Change 0.16 to thousandths.

Add a zero in the third place after the decimal point.

$$0.16 = 0.160$$

HOW TO change tenths to thousandths:

To change a decimal from tenths to thousandths, add two zeros in the second and third places after the decimal point.

EXAMPLE 3

Change 0.7 to thousandths.
Add a zero in the second and third places after the decimal point.

$$0.7 = 0.700$$

EXAMPLE 4

Be careful of a zero in the <u>first</u> place after the decimal point.

0.04 is <u>not</u> equivalent to 0.40!

0.08 is <u>not</u> equivalent to 0.80! And it's not equivalent to 008!

0.023 is <u>not</u> equivalent to 0.230!

Exercises with Hints

Change each decimal to a decimal in hundredths.
(Hint: Add a zero to the second place after the decimal point. See Example 1.)

1. 0.3 _____

2. 0.8 _____

3. 0.1 _____

4. 0.9 _____

Change each decimal to a decimal in thousandths.
(Hint: Add a zero to the third place after the decimal point, or to the second and third places. See Examples 2 and 3.)

5. 0.24 _____

6. 0.81 _____

7. 0.99 _____

8. 0.2 _____

9. 0.5 _____

10. 0.19 _____

11. 0.4 _____

12. 0.7 _____

Place these numbers in order from least to greatest.

13. 0.45, 0.4, 0.5 ____ ____ ____
(Hint: Write these numbers in hundredths.)

14. 0.721, 0.7, 0.07 ____ ____ ____
(Hint: write these numbers in thousandths.)

15. 0.08, 0.8, 0.008 ____ ____ ____
(Hint: Write these numbers in thousandths.)

Answer **T (true)** or **F (false)**.
(Hint: See Example 4.)

16. 0.5 = 0.50 _____

17. 0.2 = 0.02 _____

18. 0.8 = 0.80 _____

19. 0.670 = 0.67 _____

20. 0.44 = 0.044 _____

21. 0.091 = 0.910 _____

Solve.

22. Stan finished in second place in a 100-meter run. He came in 0.3 second after the winner. Write this time in hundredths.
(Hint: Add a zero to the second place after the decimal point.)

_____

Exercises on Your Own

Change each decimal to a decimal in hundredths.

1. 0.7 _____

2. 0.2 _____

3. 0.5 _____

4. 0.8 _____

Change each decimal to a decimal in thousandths.

5. 0.61 _____

6. 0.44 _____

7. 0.85 _____

8. 0.6 _____

9. 0.3 _____

10. 0.91 _____

11. 0.4 _____

12. 0.9 _____

Change each decimal to a decimal in hundredths.

13. 0.370 _____

14. 0.220 _____

15. 0.520 _____

Change each decimal to a decimal in tenths.

16. 0.40 _____

17. 0.20 _____

18. 0.70 _____

Answer **T (true)** or **F (false)**.

19. 0.230 = 0.23 _____

20. 0.05 = 0.5 _____

21. 0.005 = 0.05 _____

22. 0.500 = 0.5 _____

23. 0.75 = 0.750 _____

24. 0.7 = 0.07 _____

Place these numbers in order from least to greatest.

25. 0.24, 0.2, 0.024 ___ ___ ___

26. 0.05, 0.5, 0.005 ___ ___ ___

27. 0.345, 0.34, 0.3 ___ ___ ___

Solve.

28. There are 100 centimeters in a meter. So 25 centimeters is $\frac{25}{100}$ meter, or 0.25 meter. Write 25 centimeters as thousandths of a meter.

_____

29. There are 1000 milliliters in a liter. So each milliliter is $\frac{1}{1000}$ of a liter. Write 350 milliliters—

a. as a decimal in thousandths of a liter

_____

b. as a decimal in hundredths of a liter

_____

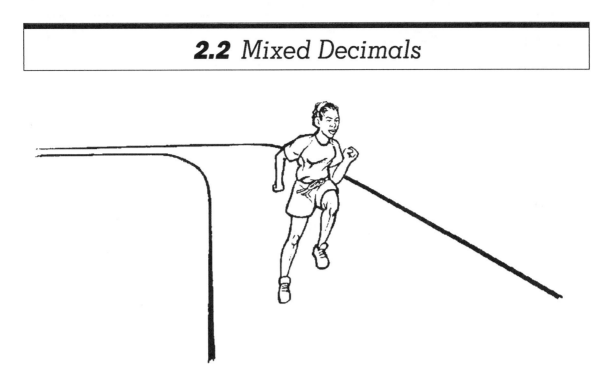

Holly said she ran $3\frac{7}{10}$ miles yesterday.

Write this mixed number as a decimal.

Read $3\frac{7}{10}$ as "3 and 7 tenths."

Write $3\frac{7}{10}$ as 3.7

The decimal point separates the whole number part from the decimal part:

Whole number	DECIMAL POINT	tenths
3	.	7

Read 3.7 the same as $3\frac{7}{10}$: "3 and 7 tenths." (Or, "3 point 7.")

$3\frac{7}{10}$ is a mixed number made up of a whole number and a fraction.

A number made up of a whole number and a decimal number is called a <u>mixed decimal</u>.

HOW TO *read mixed decimals:*

> **1.** Read the whole number part in front of the decimal point.
>
> **2.** Say "and" for the decimal point.
>
> **3.** Read the decimal part after the decimal point.

EXAMPLE 1

Write a mixed number for this mixed decimal: 27.9

Read this mixed decimal as "27 and 9 tenths."

Write 27 and 9 tenths as a mixed number.

$$27.9 = 27 \frac{9}{10}$$

EXAMPLE 2

Write a mixed number for this mixed decimal: 6.94

Remember: two places after the decimal point means hundredths.

Read 6.94 as "6 and 94 hundredths."

Write 6.94 as $6 \frac{94}{100}$:

$$6.94 = 6 \frac{94}{100}$$

EXAMPLE 3

Write a mixed number for this mixed decimal: 14.064

Three places after the decimal point means thousandths.

Read 14.064 as "14 and 64 thousandths."

Write it as $14 \frac{64}{1000}$

$$14.064 = 14 \frac{64}{1000}$$

Exercises with Hints

Choose the correct answer for each.
(Hint: Say the mixed number to yourself.)

1. $6\frac{3}{10} = ?$

   a. 6.3

   b. 6.03

   c. 6.003

2. $71\frac{23}{100} = ?$

   a. 71.023

   b. 71.23

   c. 7123

3. $2\frac{7}{1000} = ?$

   a. 2.7

   b. 2.07

   c. 2.007

Write the mixed decimal for each.
(Hint: Read the mixed number carefully. Tenths means 1 place after the decimal point. Hundredths means 2 places after the decimal point. Thousandths means 3 places after the decimal point.)

4. $7\frac{69}{100}$ _____

5. $13\frac{671}{1000}$ _____

6. $143\frac{5}{100}$ _____

7. $9000\frac{6}{10}$ _____

Write a mixed number for each.
(Hint: 2 places after the decimal point means hundredths, and 3 places means thousandths.)

8. 8.91 _____

9. 30.04 _____

10. 254.129 _____

11. 4.002 _____

Solve.

12. Ollie says that the mileage meter on his car read 34,005.1 miles. How do you read this number?
    (Hint: Mileage meters on a car read in tenths.)

    _____

13. Henry said that 10,000 meters is 6.21 miles. You can read this number as—
    (Hint: What does 2 places after the decimal point mean?)

    a. 6 and 21 tenths

    b. 6 and 21 hundredths

    c. 6 and 21 thousandths

Exercises on Your Own

Write as a mixed decimal.

1. $7\frac{1}{10}$ _____

2. $50\frac{45}{100}$ _____

3. $4\frac{372}{1000}$ _____

4. $19\frac{17}{1000}$ _____

Write as a mixed number.

5. 4.8 _____

6. 481.36 _____

7. 60.02 _____

8. 6,209.025 _____

Write a mixed decimal for each.

9. $5\frac{9}{10}$ _____

10. $14\frac{172}{1000}$ _____

11. $7,245\frac{3}{100}$ _____

12. $500\frac{5}{1000}$ _____

Solve.

13. Natali said that the mileage meter on her car reads "27,200.5 miles."

You read this number as 27 _____,

2 _____ and 5 ____ miles.

14. Monty said that his pay check was $207.56. Write this amount as

dollars and cents: ____ dollars and

____ cents.

2.3 Comparing and Ordering Mixed Decimals

Nina walked 5.4 kilometers on Monday and 5.63 kilometers on Tuesday. On which day did she walk more?

The whole number parts for 5.4 and 5.63 are both 5, so compare the decimal parts, 0.4 and 0.63.

To compare 0.4 and 0.63, make sure the decimal parts have the same number of places.

Change 0.4 to hundredths by adding a zero to the second place after the decimal point: 0.40

Compare 0.40 and 0.63:

0.40 < 0.63, so 5.4 < 5.63

Nina walked more on Tuesday.

HOW TO compare two mixed decimals:

1. Compare the whole number parts first—the mixed decimal with the greater whole number is greater.

2. If the whole number parts are equal, then compare the decimal parts.

   a. Make sure the decimal parts you are comparing have the same number of places after the decimal point.

   b. Compare the decimal parts as if they were whole numbers.

EXAMPLE 1

Which mixed number is greater, 70.04 or 7.4?

   1. Compare the whole number parts: 70 and 7.

   2. Since 70 > 7, then 70.04 > 7.4.

EXAMPLE 2

Which is greater, 7.08 or 7.8?

   1. Since the whole number parts are both 7, compare the decimal parts 0.08 and 0.8

   2. Add a zero to the second place of 0.8 so that the decimal is in hundredths—0.80

   3. Compare 0.08 and 0.80.

Since 0.80 > 0.08, then 7.8 > 7.08

EXAMPLE 3

Place these in order from least to greatest: 47.581, 48.041, 47.58.

   1. First, compare the whole number parts: 47, 48, and 47.

   2. Since 47 < 48, then the greatest number is 48.041.

   3. The other two numbers 47.581 and 47.58 have the same whole number parts. So compare the decimal parts: 0.581 and 0.58.

   4. Add a zero to the third place of 0.58 so that 0.581 and 0.58 have the same number of places—0.580

   5. Compare 0.580 and 0.581:

   0.580 <   0.581

   So 47.580 < 47.581

The numbers in order from the least to the greatest are:

47.58,   47.581,   48.041

Exercises with Hints

Which decimal is greater?
(Hint: Make sure the decimal parts have the same number of places.)

1. 0.43 or 0.437 _____

2. 0.003 or 0.030 _____

3. 0.71 or 0.7 _____

Which mixed decimal is greater?
(Hint: Make sure to check the whole number part first, then the decimal part.)

4. 15.045 or 16.043 _____

5. $9.34 or $9.67 _____

6. 1.032 or 1.32 _____

7. 2.347 or 2.343 _____

8. 17.3 or 17.32 _____

9. 145.123 or 145.1 _____

Place these decimals in order from least to greatest.
(Hint: Make sure the decimal parts have the same number of places before you order them.)

10. 3.56, 3.58, and 2.9 _____

11. 40.05, 40.5, and 40.005 _____

12. 5.571, 5.572, and 5.57 _____

13. 61.065, 61.6, and 61.06 _____

Solve.

14. Elena spent $45.36 at the supermarket on Saturday, and $45.63 on Monday. On which day did she spend more, Saturday or Monday? *(Hint: Compare dollars first, then cents.)*

_____

Exercises on Your Own

Place **<** or **>** between the decimals.

1. $0.37 ___ $0.36

2. 0.471 ___ 0.47

3. 0.2 ___ 0.25

4. 0.801 ___ 0.803

5. 0.001 ___ 0.01

6. 0.4 ___ 0.41

Place **<** or **>** between the decimal numbers.

7. 4.571 ___ 5.571

8. 9.1 ___ 9.01

9. 5.902 ___ 5.906

10. 10.332 ___ 11.331

11. 33.048 ___ 33.008

12. 7.4 ___ 7.401

Place these decimals in order from least to greatest.

13. 0.2, 0.7, and 0.1 _____

14. 0.05, 0.07, and 0.5 _____

15. 0.009, 0.09, and 0.9 _____

16. 0.002, 0.102, and 0.012 _____

Place these mixed numbers in order from least to greatest.

17. 3.1, 3.7, and 3.3 _____

18. 4.01, 4.1, and 4.5 _____

19. 17.572, 17.257, and 17.571 _____

20. 8.1, 8.02, 8.153 _____

Solve.

21. Anthony jumped these heights in a track meet for his school: 1.980 meters, 1.993 meters, and 1.989 meters. Place these heights in order from the least to the greatest.

_____

22. Alma weighed 2 batches of chemicals in her lab very carefully. The cobalt chloride weighed 2.47 grams and the sodium carbonate weighed 2.4 grams. Which weighed more, the cobalt chloride or the sodium carbonate?

_____

2.4 Reading and Writing Mixed Decimals

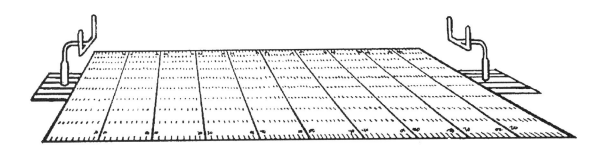

Ruth was talking to Joe on the phone. Ruth said: "I just figured out that the length of a football field, in meters, is ninety-one and forty-four hundredths meters."

Joe wrote Ruth's number as a mixed decimal.

A mixed decimal has two parts, a whole number part *and* a decimal part.

When we say or read a mixed decimal, the two parts are separated by the word *and.* The *and* stands for the decimal point.

The word *hundredths* means two decimal places.

Ninety-one *and* forty-four hundredths = 91.44

HOW TO *write a mixed decimal number:*

> *1.* Find the word *and.* It separates the whole number part from the decimal part.
>
> *2.* Write the whole number part—to the left of *and.* If there is no *and,* then there is no whole number part.
>
> *3.* Write a decimal point for *and.*
>
> *4.* Determine the number of decimal places after *and.* The number of places tells you whether the decimal part is—
>
> > tenths—1 place;
> >
> > hundredths—2 places; or
> >
> > thousandths—3 places.
>
> *5.* Write the decimal part.

EXAMPLE 1

Write the decimal number for "three hundred sixty-two and two hundred forty-six thousandths."

1. Find the word *and*.
2. Write the number before *and*:   362
3. Write the decimal point: 362.
4. The number after the decimal point is thousandths. So the decimal part is 3 places.
5. Two hundred fifty-six thousandths = .256

The mixed number is 362.256.

EXAMPLE 2

Write the decimal number for "six and three hundredths."

1. Find the word *and*.
2. Write the number before *and*: 6
3. Write the decimal point: 6.
4. The number after the decimal point is hundredths. So the decimal part is 2 places.
5. Three hundredths = .03 (not .3!)

The mixed number is 6.03.

EXAMPLE 3

How do you read 65.29?

1. The number before the decimal point is 65.
2. There are two places for the decimal part, so the decimal shows hundredths.
3. We read 65.29 as sixty-five and twenty-nine hundredths.

Exercises with Hints

Write the decimal number for each.
(Hint: There is no whole number part. The number before the decimal point is 0.)

1. twenty-five hundredths _____

2. six-hundred fifty-eight thousandths _____

3. forty hundredths _____

4. nine tenths _____

Write the mixed decimal for each.
(Hint: Find the and first, then the whole number and the decimal part.)

5. seventy-one and ninety-eight hundredths _____

6. eight hundred five and four thousandths _____

7. two hundred fifty and thirty-four thousandths _____

8. seven and seven tenths _____

Write these numbers in words.
(Hint: The word and takes the place of the decimal point.)

9. 5.3 _____

10. 17.71 _____

11. 90.07 _____

12. 0.726 _____

13. 1.065 _____

14. 49.001 _____

15. 1.45 _____

16. 44.01 _____

Solve.

17. The height of the cabinet in Felecia's kitchen is three and twenty-five hundredths feet. Write this number as a mixed decimal.
(Hint: Hundredths means 2 places after the decimal point.)

_____

Exercises on Your Own _____

Write the decimal number for each.

1. forty-two hundredths _____

2. seven tenths _____

3. five hundred sixty-three
thousandths _____

4. five hundredths _____

Write the mixed decimal for each.

5. two and five tenths _____

6. thirty-eight and seventy-five
hundredths _____

7. forty and seven hundred
fifty-nine thousandths _____

8. sixteen and nine
hundredths _____

9. six hundred and
one thousandths _____

Write these numbers in words.

10. 4.3 _____

11. 90.1 _____

12. 751.27 _____

13. 5.152 _____

14. 1.04 _____

15. 10.004 _____

16. 100.4 _____

17. 56.982 _____

Solve.

19. Craig said he weighed one hundred
twelve and four tenths pounds.
Write this number as a mixed
decimal.

_____

20. Hillary is 1.74 meters tall. Write this
number in words.

_____

21. Margo saved $306.03 in her
savings account. Write this amount
in words.

_____

Change each decimal to a decimal in hundredths.

1. 0.3 _____

2. 0.6 _____

3. 0.9 _____

Change each decimal to a decimal in thousandths.

4. 0.91 _____

5. 0.32 _____

6. 0.8 _____

Change each decimal to a decimal in hundredths.

7. 0.410 _____

8. 0.890 _____

9. 0.450 _____

Change each decimal to a decimal in tenths.

10. 0.10 _____

11. 0.80 _____

12. 0.50 _____

Answer **T (true)** or **F (false)**.

13. 0.780 = 0.78 _____

14. 0.09 = 0.090 _____

15. 0.07 = 0.007 _____

Write as a mixed decimal.

16. $12 \frac{1}{10}$ _____

17. $\frac{99}{100}$ _____

18. $400 \frac{107}{1000}$ _____

Write as a mixed number.

19. 7.9 _____

20. 30.48 _____

21. 298.007 _____

Write a mixed decimal for each.

22. $4 \frac{1}{10}$ _____

23. $41 \frac{271}{1000}$ _____

24. $3,176 \frac{9}{100}$ _____

Place < or > between the decimal numbers.

25. 0.5 ___ 0.52

26. 0.006 ___ 0.06

27. 0.932 ___ 0.937

Place < or > between the decimal numbers.

28. 9.206 ___ 7.602

29. 20.001 ___ 20.01

30. 671.083 ___ 671.081

Place these mixed numbers in order from least to greatest.

31. 27.36, 27.37, and 27.35

___ ___ ___

32. 2.78, 2.781, and 2.782

___ ___ ___

33. 10.9, 11.09, and 12.009

___ ___ ___

34. 4.8, 4.01, 4.7 ___ ___ ___

Write the mixed decimal for each.

35. five and seven tenths ___

36. seventy-seven and eighteen hundredths

___

37. ninety and four hundred twenty-two thousandths

___

38. three and four thousandths

___

How do you say these numbers?

39. 7.9 ___

40. 40.82 ___

41. 376.208 ___

Solve.

42. Julia was first in the 100-meter race by 0.7 second.

   a. Write this time in hundredths.

   ___

   b. Write this time in thousandths.

   ___

43. Flora said that she worked 4 and 25 hundredths hours more last month than this month. Write this number as a mixed number.

___

44. Watson returned from the chem lab to report that there werere $6\frac{24}{1000}$ liters of a solution left for his experiment. Write this number as a mixed decimal.

___

45. Ossie spent $267.67 in the morning, $267.55 in the afternoon, and $267.99 in the evening.

   a. In which part of the day did he spend the most money?

   ___

   b. In which part of the day did he spend the least?

   ___

46. Velma, Lien, and Maureen were the top three finishers in the diving competition. Velma received an average score of 9.93, Lien received 9.89, and Maureen received 9.95.

   a. Who came in first?   _____

   b. Who came in second? _____

47. Norma drank 2.45 liters of juice after work. Write this number in words.

_____

48. Adolfo worked seventeen and 75 hundredths hours last week. Write this number as a mixed decimal.

_____

49. Marty spent $439.07 at the mall. Write this amount in words.

_____

3. Adding Decimals

3.1 Adding With Tenths, Hundredths, and Thousandths

José walks 0.7 mile to his job in the morning. At the end of the day, he walks home a different way. The distance home is 0.9 mile. How far does he walk to and from work each day?

To find the solution, add: 0.7 + 0.9 = **?**

HOW TO add decimals:

1. Write the decimals under each other.

2. Make sure the decimal points are lined up. THIS STEP IS THE KEY TO ADDING WITH DECIMALS! If you don't line up the decimals, you'll get the wrong answer.

3. Add each place, starting at the right. Make sure your answer numbers line up, just like the decimal points do.

4. Place the decimal point in the sum lined up under the other decimal points.

Follow these steps to find the solution.

Decimals lined up

```
    0.7
+   0.9
───────
    1.6
```

Numbers lined up

Jose walks 1.6 miles to and from work each day.

EXAMPLE 1

Add: 0.94 + 0.75

$$
\begin{array}{r}
0.94 \\
+\ 0.75 \\
\hline
1.69
\end{array}
$$

EXAMPLE 2

Add: 0.591 + 0.038 + 0.629

$$
\begin{array}{r}
0.591 \\
0.038 \\
+\ 0.629 \\
\hline
1.258
\end{array}
$$

Exercises with Hints

Add these decimals in tenths.
(Hint: Write the numbers in a column. Line up the decimal points!)

1. 0.4 + 0.1 = _____

2. 0.8 + 0.7 = _____

3. 0.6 + 0.2 + 0.9 = _____

Add these decimals in hundredths.
(Hint: Add the numbers as if they were whole numbers.)

4. 0.34 + 0.08 = _____

5. 0.51 + 0.82 = _____

6. 0.55 + 0.29 + 0.02 = _____

Add these decimals in thousandths.
(Hint: Line up the decimal points.)

7. 0.491 + 0.138 = _____

8. 0.003 + 0.936 = _____

9. 0.007 + 0.038 + 0.974 =

_____

Solve.

10. Marietta paid $.25 for a newspaper and $.67 for gum. How much money did she pay altogether? *(Hint: Add the numbers as if they were whole numbers.)*

_____

Exercises on Your Own _____

Add these decimals in tenths.

1. 0.3 + 0.2 = _____

2. 0.8 + 0.2 + 0.7 = _____

3. 0.4 + 0.5 + 0.9 + 0.2 = _____

Add these decimals in hundredths.

4. 0.38 + 0.66 = _____

5. 0.15 + 0.27 + 0.55 = _____

6. 0.44 + 0.29 + 0.03 + 0.09 =

_____

Add these decimals in thousandths.

7. 0.343 + 0.839 = _____

8. 0.003 + 0.093 + 0.528 =

_____

9. 0.251 + 0.519 + 0.012 + 0.007 =

_____

Solve.

10. At a supermarket, Juan weighed his take-out salad before he got to the checkout counter. It weighed 0.5 pound. Then he added 0.2 pound more. How much did his salad weigh then?

_____

3.2 Adding Mixed Decimals

Gil drove 5.3 miles on Monday and 6.1 miles on Tuesday. How far did he drive altogether on these two days?

To find the solution, add these mixed numbers: 5.3 + 6.1.

```
    5.3
+   6.1
_____
```

HOW TO *add mixed decimals:*

---

1. Write the mixed decimals under each other.

2. Make sure the decimal points are lined up.

3. Add each place, starting at the right.

4. Place the decimal point in the sum, lined up under the other decimal points.

As you see, adding mixed decimals is the same as adding ordinary decimals.

Follow these steps to find the solution.

Step 1	*Step 2*	*Step 3*	*Step 4*
5.3	5.3	5.3	5.3
+ 6.1	+ 6.1	+ 6.1	+ 6.1
		11 4	11.4

Gil ran 11.4 miles on Monday and Tuesday.

EXAMPLE 1

Add: 6.03 + 17.59 = **?**

$$\begin{array}{r} 6.03 \\ +17.59 \\ \hline 23.62 \end{array}$$

EXAMPLE 2

Add: 19.047 + 2.719 + 0.001 = **?**

$$\begin{array}{r} 19.047 \\ 2.719 \\ +0.001 \\ \hline 21.767 \end{array}$$

Exercises with Hints

Add. The decimal parts are in tenths.
(Hint: Write the mixed decimals under each other.)

1. 2.7 + 3.9 = _____

2. 6.1 + 0.8 = _____

3. 15.9 + 9.5 + 22.7 = _____

Add. The decimal parts are in hundredths.
(Hint: Line up the decimal points of the mixed decimals)

4. 14.82 + 2.41 = _____

5. 8.26 + 287.05 = _____

6. 21.99 + 3.76 + 80.65 = _____

Add. The decimal parts are in thousandths.
(Hint: Add the numbers as if they were whole numbers.)

7. 2.762 + 15.054 = _____

8. 94.895 + 1.083 + 8.001 =

_____

9. 300.003 + 1.452 = _____

Solve.

10. After work, Gabe drove 5.1 miles to the dentist. Then he drove 3.8 miles home. How far did he drive?
(Hint: Add each place, starting at the right.)

_____

Exercises on Your Own

Add.

1. 0.4 + 0.5 = _____

2. 1.6 + 3.9 = _____

3. 0.58 + 0.87 = _____

4. 1.87 + 10.06 = _____

5. 0.984 + 0.385 = _____

6. 40.295 + 7.048 = _____

7. 3.2 + 7.8 + 10.6 = _____

8. 13.02 + 2.38 + 5.91 = _____

9. 8.154 + 25.003 = _____

10. 6.026 + 3.004 + 200.527 =

_____

Solve.

11. The diner in Marlo's town charged $4.50 for a tuna sandwich and $.85 for milk. How much would a tuna sandwich and milk cost?

_____

3.3 Adding Mixed Numbers: Writing Zeros

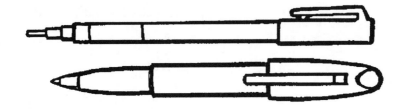

Mira measured her two pens. The red one is 5.73 inches long, and the green one is 6.2 inches long. What is the length of the two pens when they are placed end-to-end?

To find the solution, add 5.73 and 6.2.

1. Write the addition problem the way you learned in the last lesson, with the decimal points one above the other.

$$\begin{array}{r} 5.73 \\ + 6.2 \\ \hline \end{array}$$

2. Write a zero after the 2 to fill in the hundredths place.

$$\begin{array}{r} 5.73 \\ + 6.2\mathbf{0} \\ \hline \end{array}$$

Now both decimal numbers have the same number of decimal places.

3. Add the two numbers, and

4. Place the decimal point in the sum directly under the other decimal points.

$$\begin{array}{r} 5.73 \\ + 6.20 \\ \hline 11.93 \end{array}$$

Mira's pens measure 11.93 inches end-to-end.

Step 2 is a new step in the method for adding mixed decimals.

HOW TO *add mixed decimals:*

1. Write the mixed decimals under each other. Make sure the decimal points are lined up.

2. Write zeros to fill in the places.

3. Add in the usual way, starting at the right.

4. Place the decimal point in the sum under the other decimal points.

EXAMPLE 1

Add: 7.2 + 1.783.

1. Set up the problem:

$$\begin{array}{r} 7.2 \\ +\ 1.783 \\ \hline \end{array}$$

2, 3, and 4. Write zeros to fill in the missing hundredths and thousandths places, add, and put in the decimal point.

$$\begin{array}{r} 7.200 \\ +\ 1.783 \\ \hline 8.983 \end{array}$$

EXAMPLE 2

Add: 28.007 + 4.8 + 235.75

1. Set up the problem:

$$\begin{array}{r} 28.007 \\ 4.8 \\ +\ 235.75 \\ \hline \end{array}$$

2, 3, and 4. Write zeros to fill in the missing decimal places, add, and put in the decimal point.

$$\begin{array}{r} 28.007 \\ 4.800 \\ +\ 235.750 \\ \hline 268.557 \end{array}$$

Exercises with Hints

Add.

(Hint: Write zeros to fill in the hundredths places.)

1. 5.3 + 7.14 = _____

2. 3.1 + 30.01 = _____

3. 700.01 + 7.1 = _____

4. 1.1 + 7.93 + 6.9 = _____

Add.

(Hint: Write zeros to fill in the thousandths places.)

5. 4.917 + 34.73 = _____

6. 48.02 + 17.452 = _____

7. 13.002 + 3.05 = _____

8. 4.51 + 2.276 + 9.13 = _____

Add.

(Hint: Write zeros to fill in the hundredths and thousandths places.)

9. 7.8 + 2.37 + 45.903 = _____

10. 328.1 + 5.9 + 4.002 = _____

Solve.

11. Vince measured the lengths of two cables. They measured 5.7 meters and 4.65 meters. How long were they together?
(Hint: Write a zero to fill in the hundredths place.)

_____

Exercises on Your Own _____

Add.

1. 4.9 + 2.67 = _____

2. 407.23 + 1.1 = _____

3. 13.721 + 56.8 = _____

4. 4.087 + 17.843 + 2.5 = _____

5. 307.3 + 3.008 = _____

6. 38.9 + 1.273 = _____

7. 4.86 + 8.4 + 9.581 = _____

8. 387.4 + 1.255 + 9.02 = _____

9. 7.1 + 300.003 = _____

10. 45.23 + 761.6 + 4.918 = _____

Solve.

11. According to a computer analysis, Nicholas worked 35.205 hours during the first week of September. He worked 32.7 hours during the second week of September. How many hours did he work for the two weeks?

_____

12. Ruth's average during the first half of the season was 7.3 points. Carla scored 9.24 points. What is the sum of these averages?

_____

3.4 Adding Mixed Decimals: Writing Decimal Points and Zeros after Whole Numbers

Kurt bicycled 18.36 miles for one hour and 14 miles for a second hour. How many miles did he bicycle in the two hours?

To find the answer, add: 18.36 + 14

$$
\begin{array}{r}
18.36 \\
+\ 14 \\
\hline
\end{array}
$$

Write a decimal point after the whole number.

$$
\begin{array}{r}
18.36 \\
+\ 14. \\
\hline
\end{array}
$$

Write zeros to fill in the tenths and hundredths places.

Then add.

$$
\begin{array}{r}
18.36 \\
+\ 14.00 \\
\hline
32.36
\end{array}
$$

Kurt bicycled 32.36 miles in two hours.

HOW TO *add whole numbers and decimal numbers:*

1. Write a decimal point after each whole number.
2. Write zeros in the decimal places after the decimal point.
3. If necessary, write zeros to fill in all other decimal places.
4. Add the numbers.

EXAMPLE 1

Add: 35 + 2.927

$$
\begin{array}{r}
35 \\
+\ 2.927 \\
\hline
\end{array}
$$

Step 1   *Step 2*   *(Step 3 not needed)*

$$
\begin{array}{r}
35. \\
+\ 2.927 \\
\hline
\end{array}
$$

$$
\begin{array}{r}
35.\mathbf{000} \\
+\ 2.927 \\
\hline
\end{array}
$$

Step 4

$$
\begin{array}{r}
35.000 \\
+\ 2.927 \\
\hline
37.927
\end{array}
$$

EXAMPLE 2

Add: 6.7 + 421 + 35.091

$$
\begin{array}{r}
6.7 \\
421 \\
+\ 35.091 \\
\hline
\end{array}
$$

Step 1   *Step 2*   *Step 3*

$$
\begin{array}{r}
6.7 \\
421. \\
+\ 35.091 \\
\hline
\end{array}
$$

$$
\begin{array}{r}
6.7 \\
421.\mathbf{000} \\
+\ 35.091 \\
\hline
\end{array}
$$

$$
\begin{array}{r}
6.7\mathbf{00} \\
421.000 \\
+\ 35.091 \\
\hline
\end{array}
$$

Step 4

$$
\begin{array}{r}
6.700 \\
421.000 \\
+\ 35.091 \\
\hline
462.791
\end{array}
$$

Exercises with Hints

Add.
(Hint: Write zeros to fill in the tenths places.)

1. $5 + 2.7 =$ _____

2. $3.9 + 47 =$ _____

3. $17 + 5.5 =$ _____

4. $6.4 + 2.9 + 94 =$ _____

Add.
(Hint: Write zeros to fill in the tenths and hundredths places.)

5. $17.43 + 85 =$ _____

6. $482.74 + 4 =$ _____

7. $300 + 42.05 =$ _____

8. $3.61 + 2.06 + 67 =$ _____

Add.
(Hint: Write zeros to fill in the tenths, hundredths, and thousandths places.)

9. $17.361 + 9 =$ _____

10. $2.016 + 328 =$ _____

11. $521.981 + 13 + 8 =$ _____

12. $1.005 + 32.072 + 8 =$ _____

Solve.

13. Teri made $38.56 last week at the fast food restaurant where she works, and she made $50 this week. How much did she make in the two weeks?
(Hint: Write zeros in the tenths and the hundredths places.)

_____

14. Judd received these scores on three parts of a test: 23.2, 38, and 38.92. What was his total score?
(Hint: Write zeros to fill in the tenths and hundredths places.)

_____

Exercises on Your Own _____

Add.

1. $3.6 + 98 =$ _____

2. $76 + 3.5 + 2.9 =$ _____

3. $45.12 + 7 =$ _____

4. $2.56 + 501 + 83 =$ _____

5. $904 + 72.128 =$ _____

6. $12.481 + 243.402 + 17 =$

_____

7. $9.23 + 6.551 + 45 =$ _____

8. $2 + 4.8 + 2.01 + 3.047 =$

_____

9. $14 + 2.007 + 4.7 =$ _____

10. $4.07 + 9.3 + 1.872 + 5 =$

_____

11. $800 + 2.815 =$ _____

12. $4.5 + 2.77 + 1.825 =$ _____

Solve.

13. The bill for repairing Celia's car came to $59 and the bill for gasoline came to $12.94. How much did she have to pay altogether?

_____

14. The dining room floor in Roberta's house is 17.3 feet long. The width of this dining room is 12.82 feet. What is the total length and width?

_____

3.5 Review

Add these decimals in tenths.

1. 0.6 + 0.2 = _____

2. 0.4 + 0.9 + 0.7 = _____

3. 0.3 + 0.2 + 0.8 + 0.5 =_____

Add these decimals or amounts.

4. $.45 + $.84 = _____

5. 0.65 + 0.07 + 0.92 = _____

6. 0.88 + 0.17 + 0.05 + 0.19 = _____

Add these decimals in thousandths.

7. 0.277 + 0.603 = _____

8. 0.045 + 0.814 + 0.609 =

_____

9. 0.541 + 0.276 + 0.228 + 0.008 =

_____

Add.

10. 7.4 + 3.8 = _____

11. $12.78 + $14.82 = _____

12. 33.857 + 2.782 = _____

13. 36.879 + 903.276 + 5.003 =

_____

14. 0.206 + 452 = _____

Add.

15. 8.9 + 3.48 = _____

16. 305.59 + 46.4 = _____

17. 6.105 + 24.5 = _____

18. 14.065 + 6.65 + 9.1 =

_____

19. 287.68 + 2.7 + 17.185 =

_____

Add.

20. 14.3 + 43 = _____

21. 67 + 3.504 + 17 = _____

22. 5.206 + 73 = _____

23. 26.65 + 328 + 45.3 = _____

24. 488 + 33.692 = _____

25. 288.5 + 398.28 + 90 = _____

26. 9 + 614 + 45.5 = _____

27. 8.004 + 7 + 13.98 + 7.22 =

_____

Solve.

28. Rodney spent $.33 before school, $.76 during the school day, and $.92 after school. How much money did he spend all day?

_____

29. Geraldo brought three envelopes to the post office. One weighed 0.3 pound, another weighed 0.6 pound, and the third weighed 0.8 pound. How much did the three envelopes weigh altogether?

_____

30. Mildred added up the income from her hat shop over the past four days: Monday: $298.76; Tuesday: $732.45; Wednesday: $794.77; and Thursday: $2098.05. What was the total income over these four days?

_____

31. Tanya filled the tank of her car twice on the trip to Canada. The first time the car took 14.76 gallons and the second time 14.3 gallons. What is the total amount of gasoline that she bought?

_____

32. Paco weighed two packages of cheese before he computed their price. One package weighed 2.4 kilograms and the other weighed 1.275 kilograms. What was the total weight of the two packages?

_____

33. Sam spent $13.67 for breakfast and $26 for dinner when he went on a trip for his company. His hotel bill was $126.87. What was the total of the two meals and the hotel?

_____

34. Donald ran around the track four times. These were his times: 23.67 seconds; 22.6 seconds; 27.7 seconds; and 22.75 seconds. How many seconds did it take him to complete the four laps?

_____

4. Subtracting Decimals

4.1 Subtracting With Tenths, Hundredths, and Thousandths

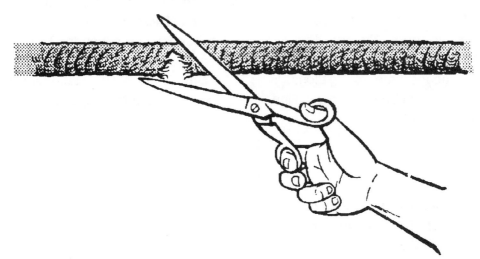

From a piece of rope 0.9 meter long, Henry cuts a piece measuring 0.3 meter. How long is the piece that remains?

To find the solution, subtract:

$$0.9 - 0.3 = ?$$

HOW TO *subtract decimals:*

> **1.** Write the decimals under each other.
>
> **2.** Make sure the decimal points are lined up.
>
> **3.** Subtract in each place, starting at the right.
>
> **4.** Place the decimal point in the difference under the other decimal points. (The difference is the name for the answer.)

Follow these steps to find the solution.

```
  0.9
- 0.3
-----
  0.6
```

The length of rope left is 0.6 meter long.

EXAMPLE 1

Subtracting decimals in hundredths follows the same basic steps as above.

Subtract: 0.85 – 0.24 = **?**

$$\begin{array}{r} 0.85 \\ -\ 0.24 \\ \hline 0.61 \end{array}$$

EXAMPLE 2

Subtract: 0.805 – 0.274

$$\begin{array}{r} 0.805 \\ -\ 0.274 \\ \hline 0.531 \end{array}$$

Exercises with Hints

Subtract.

(Hint: Just follow the steps in the "How To" Section, above.)

1. 0.8 – 0.2 = _____

2. 0.9 – 0.6 = _____

3. 0.6 – 0.1 = _____

4. 0.7 – 0.6 = _____

Subtract.

(Hint: Subtract in the tenths and hundredths places. Follow Example 1.)

5. 0.79 – 0.25 = _____

6. 0.92 – 0.58 = _____

7. 0.60 – 0.48 = _____

8. 0.53 – 0.08 = _____

Subtract.

(Hint: Subtract in the tenths, hundredths, and thousandths places. Follow Example 2.)

9. 0.772 – 0.234 = _____

10. 0.284 – 0.163 = _____

11. 0.507 – 0.397 = _____

12. 0.276 – 0.047 = _____

Solve.

13. Pedro came in second place in a 100-yard dash. His time was 0.45 seconds slower than the winner of the race. Jonathan came in third, and his time was 0.92 second slower than the winner. How long after Pedro did Jonathan finish?
(Hint: Follow the steps in the "How To" Section. As usual, make sure that everything lines up.)

_____

14. Christa used two kinds of nails to fix her back porch. One type was 0.9 inch long. The other type was 0.7 inch long. How much longer is the 0.9 inch nail?
(Hint: Follow the steps in the "How To" Section.)

_____

Exercises on Your Own _____

Subtract.

1. $0.6 - 0.4 =$ _____

2. $0.93 - 0.62 =$ _____

3. $0.618 - 0.192 =$ _____

4. $0.72 - 0.46 =$ _____

5. $0.179 - 0.025 =$ _____

6. $0.902 - 0.058 =$ _____

7. $0.09 - 0.01 =$ _____

8. $0.5 - 0.5 =$ _____

9. $0.804 - 0.781 =$ _____

10. $0.38 - 0.09 =$ _____

11. $0.003 - 0.001 =$ _____

12. $0.071 - 0.005 =$ _____

Solve.

13. Charlotte lives 0.8 mile from the bank and 0.4 mile from the post office. How much further is her house from the bank than from the post office?

_____

14. Bill has $.45 and needs $.98 to buy his favorite chewing gum. How much more money does he need?

_____

4.2 Subtracting Mixed Decimals

Mandy ran 7.3 miles on Friday and 5.9 miles on Saturday. How much further did he run on Friday than on Saturday?

To find the solution, subtract: 7.3 − 5.9

$$\begin{array}{r} 7.3 \\ -\ 5.9 \\ \hline \end{array}$$

HOW TO subtract mixed decimals:

1. Write the mixed decimals under each other.
2. Make sure the decimal points are lined up.
3. Subtract in each place, starting at the right.
4. Place the decimal point in the difference under the other decimal points.

Follow these steps to find the solution.

Step 1	Step 2	Step 3	Step 4

$$\begin{array}{r} 7.3 \\ -\ 5.9 \\ \hline \end{array} \qquad \begin{array}{r} 7.3 \\ -\ 5.9 \\ \hline \end{array} \qquad \begin{array}{r} 7.3 \\ -\ 5.9 \\ \hline 1\ 4 \end{array} \qquad \begin{array}{r} 7.3 \\ -\ 5.9 \\ \hline 1.4 \end{array}$$

Mandy ran 1.4 miles more on Friday than on Saturday.

EXAMPLE 1

Subtract: 13.96 – 7.58 = **?**

$$\begin{array}{r} 13.96 \\ -\ 7.58 \\ \hline 6.38 \end{array}$$

EXAMPLE 2

Subtract: 27.057 – 15.528 = **?**

$$\begin{array}{r} 27.057 \\ -\ 15.528 \\ \hline 11.529 \end{array}$$

Exercises with Hints

Subtract.
(Hint: The decimal parts are in tenths.)

1. 5.8 – 1.9 = _____

2. 6.3 – 1.5 = _____

3. 12.7 – 5.2 = _____

Subtract.
(Hint: The decimal parts are in hundredths.)

4. 16.37 – 6.94 = _____

5. 14.87 + 7.07 = _____

6. 402.33 – 9.76 = _____

Subtract.
(Hint: The decimal parts are in thousandths.)

7. 45.217 – 22.025 = _____

8. 207.115 – 45.669 = _____

9. 3.604 – 0.038 = _____

Solve.

10. Bob started the day with $45.75. He spent $32.87. How much did he have left?
(Hint: Write the decimals under each other, and follow the steps of the "How To" section.)

_____

11. Harriet used to weigh 56.7 kilograms. She went on a diet and lost 2.8 kilograms. How much does she weigh now?
(Hint: Follow the steps of the "How To" section.)

_____

Exercises on Your Own _____

Subtract.

1. $0.6 - 0.6 =$ _____

2. $0.38 - 0.17 =$ _____

3. $6.7 - 3.4 =$ _____

4. $27.91 - 15.47 =$ _____

5. $2.07 - 1.45 =$ _____

7. $0.582 - 0.388 =$ _____

8. $503.008 - 275.549 =$ _____

9. $653.2 - 27.8 =$ _____

10. $3.2 - 0.7 =$ _____

11. $9.9 - 4.3 =$ _____

12. $1.73 - 0.44 =$ _____

Solve.

13. Rich drove 34.75 miles to get to a concert and 28.88 miles to get back home. How many more miles did he drive to get to the concert than to return home?

_____

14. The printout in Rafael's office computer says that there are still 3.924 tons of supplies in the warehouse. Last month there were 4.027 tons of supplies in the warehouse. How much more was there last month?

_____

15. The scale showed that Clement weighs 165.8 pounds. His sister weighs 104.3 pounds. How much more does Clement weigh?

_____

4.3 Subtracting Mixed Numbers: Writing Zeros

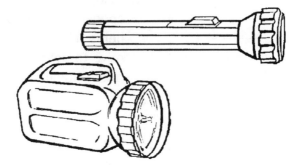

Kal has two flashlights. The thin one is 6.3 inches long. The fat one is 4.94 inches long. How much longer is the thin flashlight?

To find the solution, subtract: 6.3 − 4.94

Subtract by using the method of Lesson 2 of this chapter.

$$\begin{array}{r} 6.3 \\ -\,4.94 \\ \hline \end{array}$$

Write a zero after 3 to fill in the hundredths place.

$$\begin{array}{r} 6.3\mathbf{0} \\ -\,4.94 \\ \hline \end{array}$$

Now both decimal numbers have the same number of decimal places.

Subtract and place the decimal point in the sum:

$$\begin{array}{r} 6.30 \\ -\,4.94 \\ \hline 1.36 \end{array}$$

The thin flashlight is 1.36 inches longer than the fat one.

HOW TO subtract mixed decimals:

1. Write the mixed decimals under each other.
2. Make sure the decimal points are lined up.
3. **Write zeros to fill in the places.**
4. Subtract in each place, starting at the right.
5. Place the decimal point in the difference under the other decimal points.

Step 3 is a new step in the method for subtracting mixed decimals.

EXAMPLE 1

Subtract: 17.82 - 4.9 = **?**

$$17.82$$
$$-\ \ 4.9$$

Write a zero after 9 to fill in the hundredths place.

$$17.82$$
$$-\ \ 4.9\mathbf{0}$$
$$\overline{12.92}$$

EXAMPLE 2

Subtract: 9.2 - 5.406 = **?**

$$9.2$$
$$-\ 5.406$$

Write zeros to fill in the hundredths and thousandths places.

$$9.2\mathbf{00}$$
$$-\ 5.406$$
$$\overline{3.794}$$

Exercises with Hints

Subtract.
(Hint: Write zeros to fill in the hundredths places.)

1. 4.1 – 1.87 = _____

2. 58.38 – 1.7 = _____

3. 745.08 – 251.7 = _____

4. 8.6 – 3.05 = _____

Subtract.
(Hint: Write zeros to fill in the thousandths places.)

5. 45.95 – 22.112 = _____

6. 5.036 – 1.48 = _____

7. 26.008 – 0.72 = _____

8. 482.04 – 26.438 = _____

Subtract.

(Hint: Write zeros to fill in the hundredths and thousandths places.)

9. $7.3 - 3.081 =$ _____

10. $84.729 - 42.8 =$ _____

11. $84.003 - 36.6 =$ _____

12. $4.4 - 0.238 =$ _____

Solve.

13. After the sun, the star that is closest to the earth is Proxima Centauri. It is 4.2 light years away. The next closest star is Alpha Centauri, which is 4.35 light years away. How much farther away is Alpha Centauri than Proxima Centauri?
(Hint: You need to write a zero to fill in the hundredths place for Proxima Centauri.)

_____

Exercises on Your Own

Subtract.

1. $38.44 - 11.1 =$ _____

2. $402.834 - 231.7 =$ _____

3. $4.701 - 0.9 =$ _____

4. $54.915 - 48.07 =$ _____

5. $7.2 - 3.62 =$ _____

6. $60.5 - 2.007 =$ _____

7. $18.38 - 10.671 =$ _____

8. $55.083 - 27.835 =$ _____

9. $3.804 - 0.629 =$ _____

10. $37.056 - 9.27 =$ _____

11. $100.7 - 98.002 =$ _____

12. $981.4 - 3.206 =$ _____

Solve.

13. The Daytona Speedway is 2.5 miles long. The Talledega Super-speedway is 2.66 miles long. How much longer is the Talledega Speedway than the Daytona Speedway?

_____

14. Greg estimates that his umbrellas last 1.5 years, and that his shoes last 2.75 years. How much longer do his shoes last than his umbrellas?

_____

4.4 Subtracting Mixed Numbers: Writing Decimal Points for Whole Numbers

Larry set a new school record by jumping 8 meters. The old record was 7.27 meters. By how much did Larry beat the old record?

To find the answer, subtract: 8 – 7.27.

$$\begin{array}{r} 8 \\ -\ 7.27 \\ \hline \end{array}$$

Write a decimal point after the whole number so that the decimals line up:

$$\begin{array}{r} 8\mathbf{.} \\ -\ 7.27 \\ \hline \end{array}$$

Write zeros to fill in the tenths and hundredths places.

Then subtract.

$$\begin{array}{r} 8\mathbf{.00} \\ -\ 7.27 \\ \hline 0.73 \end{array}$$

Larry beat the old record by 0.73 meters.

HOW TO subtract whole numbers and decimal numbers:

> *1.* Write a decimal point after the whole number.
>
> *2.* Write zeros in the decimal places after the decimal point.
>
> *3.* Then subtract as usual.

EXAMPLE 1

Subtract: 47 – 8.325

Step 1	*Step 2*	*Step 3*
47.	47.**000**	47.000
– 8.325	– 8.325	– 8.325
————	————	39.675

EXAMPLE 2

Subtract: 72.057 – 46

Step 1	*Step 2*	*Step 3*
72.057	72.057	72.057
– 46.	– 46.**000**	– 46.000
————	————	26.057

Exercises with Hints

Subtract. *(Hint: Write zeros to fill in the tenths places.)*

1. 9 – 6.7 = _____

2. 43 – 2.9 = _____

3. 10.7 – 3 = _____

Subtract.
(Hint: Write zeros to fill in the tenths and hundredths places.)

4. $245 – $122.73 = _____

5. 80 – 3.56 = _____

6. 13.43 – 8 = _____

Subtract.
(Hint: Write zeros to fill in the tenths, hundredths, and thousandths places.)

7. 12 – 4.715 = _____

8. 300 – 4.206 = _____

9. 321 – 1.134 = _____

Solve.

10. Harry saw two radios that he liked. One cost $45.65 and the other cost $80. What was the difference in price between the two radios? *(Hint: Write zeros to fill in the tenths and hundredths places of the $80.)*

_____

11. Janice jumped 2.427 meters to win a standing broad jump. Her teammate Donna jumped 2.3 meters. How much farther did Janice jump? *(Hint: Write zeros to fill in the tenths and hundredths places of Donna's jump.)*

_____

Exercises on Your Own

Subtract.

1. 6 – 4.65 = _____

2. 48 – 4.7 = _____

3. $9.08 – $2 = _____

4. 427.428 – 10 = _____

5. 73 – 52.651 = _____

6. 2 – 0.603 = _____

7. 9.57 – 1.8 = _____

8. 305 – 2.403 = _____

9. $48 – $2.07 = _____

10. 12.56 – 3.927 = _____

11. 442.9 – 18.777 = _____

12. 9.004 – 6 = _____

13. 10 – 4.051 = _____

14. 437 – 12.305 = _____

Solve.

15. Thelma read the thermometer on Tuesday. It read 87.4 degrees. On Wednesday, the thermometer read 89 degrees. How many degrees warmer was it on Wednesday than Tuesday?

_____

16. Skippy averages 16 calls per week. Her friend Carla averages 5.625 calls per week. How many more calls per week does Skippy get?

_____

Subtract.

1. 0.7 – 0.2 = _____

2. $.48 – $.32 = _____

3. 0.873 – 0.407 = _____

4. 0.298 – 0.180 = _____

5. 0.013 – 0.002 = _____

6. 0.125 – 0.073 = _____

7. $.05 – $.02 = _____

8. 0.258 – 0.258 = _____

Subtract.

9. 9.2 – 2.9 = _____

10. $35.99 – $27.74 = _____

11. 33.76 – 28.45 = _____

12. 6.682 – 4.106 = _____

13. 75.105 – 67.082 = _____

14. 386.097 – 115.228 = _____

15. $206.37 – $55.62 = _____

16. 66.2 – 10.7 = _____

Subtract.

17. 42.48 – 22.7 = _____

18. 98.451 – 71.6 = _____

19. 8.023 – 0.7 = _____

20. 39.892 – 25.03 = _____

21. 8.1 – 4.08 = _____

22. 58.3 – 1.008 = _____

23. 56.908 – 37.8 = _____

24. 452.7 – 125.307 = _____

Subtract.

25. $18 – $12.22 = _____

26. 3 – 1.7 = _____

27. 17.04 – 12 = _____

28. 704.226 – 125 = _____

29. 1300 – 1000.6 = _____

30. 9 – 0.361 = _____

31. 9.57 – 1.8 = _____

32. 8.036 – 4 = _____

Solve.

33. Linda calculated that a pack of chewing gum costs her store $.09. She sells each pack for $.18. What is her net gain from the sale of a pack of chewing gum?

_____

34. Damon said that he measured the capacity of a new soft drink container as exactly as he could. He measured it twice. The first time he measured it, it was 0.658 liter. The next time it was 0.671 liter. What is the difference between the two measures?

_____

35. Ernesto's income last month was $2983.56 and his expenses were $2672.15. How much more was his income than his expenses?

_____

36. Ruth is in charge of producing a model robot for her company. One of her standards is that the robot must be able to make a full turn in 2.37 seconds. At the present time, the model robot can make a full turn in 2.88 seconds. By how much is the robot over the standard?

_____

37. The average life of a disk drive, according to a computer journal, is 2.56 years. The average life of a printer is 3.1 years. How much longer is the average life of a printer than a disk drive?

_____

38. The results of the "cafeteria test" are in. According to food experts, the average student in high school drinks 1.6 liters of soda each day and 0.575 liters of milk. How much more soda than milk does the average student drink each day?

_____

39. The calculators that Jeff wants to order come in two prices. One price is $28.66 and the other is $19. What is the difference in the prices between these two calculators?

_____

40. Jeannette predicted that the winner's time in a race would be 22 seconds. The actual time was 22.094 second. How much off was her prediction?

_____

5. Rounding and Estimating with Decimals

5.1 Rounding to the Nearest Whole Number

Connie measured her living room and found it to be 5.2 meters long. Round this length to the nearest whole number.

   5.2 is between two whole numbers: 5 and 6.
   Look at the decimal part: 0.2.
   Since 0.2 is less than 0.5, round down to the <u>lower</u> whole number.

   5.2 is rounded to 5.

The living room is <u>about</u> 5 meters long.

HOW TO *round to the nearest whole number:*

1. If the decimal part is **less than 0.5**, then round **down** to the **lower** whole number. (This means just dropping the decimal part of the number.)

2. If the decimal part is **0.5 or greater,** then round **up** to the **higher** whole number. (This means dropping the decimal part and then adding 1. You get the next higher whole number.)

EXAMPLE 1—*Decimal Part Less Than 0.5*

Round 38.2 to the nearest whole number.

Since 0.2 < 0.5, then 38.2 rounds down to 38.

EXAMPLE 2—*Decimal Part Greater Than 0.5*

Round 94.62 to the nearest whole number.

Is 0.62 greater or less than 0.5? Rewrite 0.5 as 0.50.

Since 0.62 > 0.50, then 94.62 rounds up to 95.

EXAMPLE 3—*Decimal Part Equal to 0.5*

Round 29.5 to the nearest whole number.

Since the decimal part equals 0.5, then 29.5 rounds up to 30.

EXAMPLE 4—*Rounding Dollars and Cents*

Round $45.91 to the nearest dollar.

You round dollars and cents the way you round any mixed decimal.

$45.91 is 45 dollars and 91 cents.

Since 91 cents is greater than 50 cents, round to the next higher dollar.

$45.91 rounds to $46.

Exercises with Hints

Put a check mark after each of the following numbers with a decimal part <u>greater than</u> 0.5.
(Hint: The decimal part comes after the decimal point. Remember that 0.50 is equivalent to 0.5)

1. 4.7 _____

2. 30.2 _____

3. $44.81 _____

4. 105.4 _____

5. 500.3 _____

6. $85.04 _____

7. $391.49 _____

8. 0.6 _____

In which example is the decimal part <u>equal to</u> 0.5?
(Hint: 0.50 is equivalent to 0.5)

9. 50.4 _____

10. 14.5 _____

11. $19.05 _____

12. $72.50 _____

Round to the nearest whole number.
(Hint: Use the two "How to" rules above.)

13. 4.7 _____

14. 52.5 _____

15. 17.82 _____

16. 90.09 _____

Round to the nearest dollar.
(Hint: Remember that rounding to the nearest dollar is like rounding any mixed decimal to the nearest whole number.)

17. $95.54 _____

18. $27.47 _____

19. $185.05 _____

20. $88.50 _____

Solve.

21. Koko said she weighed 46.38 kilograms. Round her weight to the nearest whole number.
(Hint: Compare the decimal part to 0.50, and use the two rules.)

_____

22. The bridge in Don's village is 847.5 meters long. Round this length to the nearest whole number.
(Hint: Use the two rules.)

_____

Exercises on Your Own

What is the decimal part for each mixed decimal?

1. $45.08 _____

2. 105.001 _____

3. 2.59 _____

4. 1.12 _____

For which mixed number is the decimal part greater than 0.5?

5. 2.8 _____

6. 1.08 _____

7. 100.4 _____

8. 62.602 _____

Round to the nearest whole number

9. 487.2 _____

10. 1.276 _____

11. 7.5 _____

12. 20.49 _____

13. 0.82 _____

14. 8.6 _____

15. 299.5 _____

16. 80.005 _____

Round to the nearest dollar.

17. $49.52 _____

18. $21.38 _____

19. $99.50 _____

20. $200.49 _____

Solve.

21. Juan found a pair of athletic shoes that he liked. They cost $65.82. Round this amount to the nearest dollar.

_____

22. Paula drank 2.7 liters of orange juice after the basketball game. Round this amount to the nearest whole number.

_____

5.2 Estimating Sums and Differences to the Nearest Whole Number

Greg bought three things at the mall.

He bought:

- a pair of running shoes for $87.25,

- a CD for $15.50,

- and a pair of sunglasses for $5.48.

Estimate how much he paid for all these items.

To estimate the cost of the three items, first round each amount to the nearest dollar:

$87.25 rounds to $87

$15.50 rounds to $16

$ 5.68 rounds to $6

Then add the rounded amounts:

$$
\begin{array}{r}
\$87 \\
16 \\
+6 \\
\hline
\$109
\end{array}
$$

Greg paid about $109 for his three purchases at the mall.

HOW TO *estimate sums and differences for mixed decimals:*

1. Round each number to the nearest whole number.
2. Add or subtract the rounded numbers.

EXAMPLE 1 —Estimating Sums

Estimate the sum: 34.87 + 29.5 + 762.48 = **?**

Round 34.87 to 35; round 29.5 to 30; and round 762.48 to 762.

Then add the rounded numbers:

$$
\begin{array}{r}
35 \\
30 \\
+\ 762 \\
\hline
827
\end{array}
$$

EXAMPLE 2—Estimating Differences

Estimate the difference: 356.8 – 201.3 = **?**

Round 356.8 to 357 and round 201.3 to 201.

Subtract the rounded numbers:

$$
\begin{array}{r}
357 \\
-\ 201 \\
\hline
156
\end{array}
$$

Exercises with Hints

Round these numbers to the nearest whole number. *(Hint: Is the tenths place greater than or equal to 0.5?)*

1. 6.3 _____

2. 38.9 _____

3. 70.5 _____

Estimate the sums. *(Hint: Round to nearest whole number or nearest dollar first.)*

4. 4.4 + 2.8 = _____

5. 38.5 + 29.4 = _____

6. $45.82 + $23.50 + $72.04=

_____

Estimate the differences.
(Hint: First round each number to the nearest whole number or nearest dollar.)

7. 7.5 – 2.3 = _____

8. 67.3 – 20.4 = _____

9. $49.90 – $38.28 = _____

Solve.

10. Flora said she spent $148.54 shopping for clothes and $18.45 for earrings. Estimate how much she spent. *(Hint: Round each amount to the nearest dollar and add.)*

_____

11. Lewis drove 38.6 miles to get to a conference. Martha drove 24.4 miles. Estimate how much longer Lewis' trip was.
(Hint: Round each number to the nearest whole number and subtract.)

_____

Exercises on Your Own _____

Round these numbers to the nearest whole number.

1. 4.6 _____

2. 17.5 _____

3. 200.4 _____

4. 49.8 _____

Round these amounts to the nearest dollar.

5. $56.25 _____

6. $400.75 _____

7. $44.09 _____

8. $19.50 _____

Estimate the sums and differences.

9. 8.7 - 2.5 = _____

10. 10.2 + 5.4 = _____

11. 549.72 + 200.45 = _____

12. 43.99 - 26.48 = _____

13. 20.83 - 10.55 = _____

14. 2.3 + 5.5 + 6.7 + 10.1 =

_____

Estimate by rounding to the nearest dollar.

15. $34.72 + $22.44 = _____

16. $291.28 - $287.50 = _____

17. $3.56 + $12.39 + $89.75 =

_____

Solve.

18. Dan won a race by 22.5 seconds. The person who came in second was Frank, whose time was 1 hour, 6 minutes and 32.2 seconds. What was Dan's time to the nearest second?

_____

19. Ethel collected $45.75 for a block party. Norma collected $78.25. Estimate to the nearest dollar how much more Norma collected than Ethel.

_____

5.3 Rounding to the Nearest Tenth

Tara finished a race in 11.23 seconds and Marcie finished in 12.38 seconds. Round these times to the nearest tenth.

To round to the nearest tenth, look at the hundredths place.

For 11.23: since **3** < 5, then 11.23 rounds *down* to 11.2

For 12.38: since **8** > 5, then 12.38 rounds *up* to 12.4

Tara finished the race in about 11.2 seconds and Marcie finished in about 12.4 seconds.

HOW TO round to the nearest tenth:

> *1.* If the number in the hundredths place is *less than 5*, then just drop it. (This is *rounding down*.)
>
> *2.* If the number in the hundredths place is *5 <u>or</u> greater than 5*, then drop it *and round the tenths place up* to the next higher number.

EXAMPLE 1

Round 38.46 to the nearest tenth.

The number in the hundredths place is 6.

6 > 5. So 38.46 rounds up to 38.5.

EXAMPLE 2

Round 389.25 to the nearest tenth.

The number in the hundredths place is 5.

Since 5 is the number in the hundredths place, 389.25 rounds up to 389.3.

EXAMPLE 3

Round 84.34 to the nearest tenth.

The number in the hundredths place is 4.

Since 4 < 5, then 84.34 rounds down to 84.3.

Exercises with Hints

What number is in the hundredths place?
(Hint: The hundredths place is the second place to the right of the decimal point.)

1. 34.87 _____

2. 201.61 _____

3. 44.563 _____

4. 1.083 _____

Look at the number in the hundredths place. Is it 5 or greater, or less than 5?
(Hint: Count two places to the right of the decimal point.)

5. The number in the hundredths place of 47.29 is— (Check one)

a. ____ 5 or greater

b. ____ less than 5

6. The number in the hundredths place of 200.085 is—

a. ____ 5 or greater

b. ____ less than 5

7. The number in the hundredths place of 12.93 is—

a. ____ 5 or greater

b. ____ less than 5

8. The number in the hundredths place of 5.551 is—

a. ___ 5 or greater

b. ___ less than 5

Round these to the nearest tenth.
(Hint: Follow the two rules given above. Look at the number in the hundredths place first, then decide whether to round the number in the tenths place up or down.)

9. 1.29 _____

10. 3.071 _____

11. 165.92 _____

12. 40.25 _____

Solve.

13. Dave did a problem on his calculator. The answer on the calculator was 26.724. What is this number rounded to the nearest tenth?
(Hint: Look at the number in the hundredths place. Decide whether to round the number in the tenths place up or down.)

_____

14. Julia averages 2.97 phone calls every hour. Round this number to the nearest tenth.
(Hint: When you round 0.9 up, you change the whole number to the next highest number.)

_____

Exercises on Your Own _____

What number is in the hundredths place?

1. 4.92 _____

2. 14.18 _____

3. 2.064 _____

4. 12.45 _____

Round each of these numbers to the nearest tenth.

5. 2.37 _____

6. 63.55 _____

7. 30.06 _____

8. 1.245 _____

9. 561.076 _____

10. 33.91 _____

11. 23.48 _____

12. 99.952 _____

Solve.

13. The average yearly snowfall in Anchorage, Alaska, is 68.13 in. Round this number to the nearest tenth.

_____

14. Marvella computed the gas mileage of her new car. It came out to 28.357 miles per gallon. Estimate the gas mileage to the nearest whole number.

_____

5.4 *Estimating Sums and Differences to the Nearest Tenth*

Elena brought two packages to the post office.

They weighed 12.74 pounds and 8.35 pounds.

Estimate how much the two packages weigh altogether to the nearest tenth of a pound.

To find the solution, round to the nearest tenth and add:

Round 12.74 to the nearest tenth: 12.74 ——> 12.7

Round 8.35 to the nearest tenth: 8.35 ——> 8.4

Add the two rounded numbers:

$$
\begin{array}{r}
12.7 \\
+\ \ 8.4 \\
\hline
21.1
\end{array}
$$

The two packages weighed about 21.1 pounds.

HOW TO *estimate sums and differences to the nearest tenth:*

> *1.* Round the number to the nearest tenth.
>
> *2.* Add or subtract the rounded numbers.

EXAMPLE 1—*Estimating Sums*

Estimate the sum to the nearest tenth: 403.57 + 233.14 = **?**

403.57 rounds to 403.6

233.14 rounds to 233.1

Add the rounded numbers:

$$403.6$$
$$+\ 233.1$$
$$\overline{636.7}$$

EXAMPLE 2—*Estimating Differences*

Estimate the difference to the nearest tenth: 56.238 − 25.458 = **?**

56.238 rounds to 56.2

25.458 rounds to 25.5

Subtract the rounded numbers:

$$56.2$$
$$-\ 25.5$$
$$\overline{30.7}$$

Exercises with Hints

Round to the nearest tenth.
(Hint: Is the hundredths place less than 5, greater than 5, or equal to 5?)

1. 45.72 _____

2. 903.25 _____

3. 19.95 _____

4. 2.38 _____

5. 18.98 _____

6. 428.246 _____

7. 75.19 _____

8. 34.72 _____

Estimate the sum by rounding to the nearest tenth.
(Hint: Round each number to the nearest tenth and add.)

9. 4.62 + 31.15 = _____

10. 9.84 + 1.27 = _____

Estimate the difference by rounding to the nearest tenth.
(Hint: Round each number to the nearest tenth and subtract.)

11. 59.98 - 36.82 = _____

12. 400.07 - 300.03 = _____

Solve.

13. Mario averaged 14.87 points for the basketball season. Jack averaged 12.23 points. Estimate the sum of the two averages by rounding to the nearest tenth and adding. *(Hint: remember to round each number to the nearest tenth first.)*

_____

14. Sonia measures 2.394 grams of sodium chloride and 4.058 grams of calcium chloride in her lab. About how much more calcium chloride than sodium chloride has she? Make your estimate by rounding to the nearest tenth and subtracting. *(Hint: When you round, ask the question: Is the hundredths place less than 5, or equal to 5 or more?)*

_____

Exercises on Your Own _____

Round to the nearest tenth.

1. 4.67 _____

2. 1.05 _____

3. 3.555 _____

4. 26.39 _____

Estimate the sum or difference by rounding to the nearest tenth.

5. 2.67 - 1.29 = _____

6. 34.85 - 3.27 = _____

7. 17.94 + 2.31 = _____

8. 8.882 + 2.052 = _____

9. 72.57 - 41.77 = _____

10. 7.22 - 3.95 = _____

11. 24.752 + 67.475 + 2.35 =

_____

12. 3.76 + 8.06 + 1.22 + 9.52 =

_____

Solve.

13. Tyrone has three packages. They weigh 3.76 kilograms, 9.45 kilograms, and 12.66 kilograms. Estimate how much they weigh altogether, to the nearest tenth of a kilogram.

_____

14. Leon received 28.45 percent of the vote for president of his class. Theresa received 34.87 percent. Estimate by rounding to the nearest tenth the percent they received together.

_____

Round to the nearest whole number.

1. 236.7 _____

2. 50.47 _____

3. 2764.512 _____

4. 0.7 _____

5. 43.177 _____

Round to the nearest dollar.

6. $35.88 _____

7. $89.50 _____

8. $238.49 _____

9. $0.75 _____

10. $999.99 _____

Estimate the sums and differences.
Round to the nearest whole number,
then do the math.

11. 4.7 - 2.4 = _____

12. 5.6 + 3.8 + 12.1 + 43.5 =

_____

13. 559.5 - 300.4 = _____

14. $17.46 - $12.22 = _____

15. 37.871 + 19.5 = _____

Estimate by first rounding to the nearest
dollar, then doing the math.

16. $45.26 + $88.52 = _____

17. $9.75 - $3.28 = _____

18. $400.48 + $10.94 + $99.50 =

_____

19. $92.21 - $18.55 = _____

20. $5.50 + $2.37 + $12.62 + $80.78 =

_____

Round these numbers to the nearest
tenth.

21. 41.35 _____

22. 32.48 _____

23. 98.853 _____

24. 0.471 _____

25. 91.049 _____

26. 7.09 _____

Estimate the sum or difference by first
rounding to the nearest tenth, then doing
the math.

27. 25.76 - 12.92 = _____

28. 6.58 - 1.73 = _____

30. 28.49 + 100.22 = _____

31. 84.82 + 5.925 + 2.86 =

_____

32. 127.75 - 82.48 = _____

33. 17.49 - 5.82 = _____

34. 8.26 + 1.88 + 0.48 = _____

Solve.

35. Valerie paid the bill for lunch. It came to $23.67. How much was the bill, rounded to the nearest dollar?

_____

36. The height of a rocket on the launch pad is 31.5 meters. Round the height to the nearest whole number.

_____

37. Georgio made $65.58 at the carnival selling ties. Molly made $86.33 selling earrings. About how much more did Molly make? (Round to the nearest dollar and subtract.)

_____

38. Felix drove 25.7 miles to get to the state park, and he drove 38.9 miles to get back. Estimate how many miles longer the trip back was by first rounding to the nearest whole numbers and then doing the math.

_____

39. Kiwa bought a cellular phone for $87.76. Round this amount to the nearest dime.

_____

40. Lilly computed the area of her office to be 22.65 square meters. Round this number to the nearest tenth.

_____

41. The average speed that Theo drove for the first half of the auto race was 187.44 miles per hour. Round this speed to the nearest tenth.

_____

42. In a recent poll of the employees of the Craig Tool Company, 23.87 per cent said that they smoked regularly, and 10.45 per cent said that they smoked occasionally. Estimate the sum of these percents by first rounding to the nearest tenth and then doing the math.

_____

43. Ken announced that his company's domestic retail sales represent 62.16 percent of the total sales, and that foreign retail sales represent 4.82 percent of the total sales. Estimate the sum of these percents by first rounding to the nearest tenth and then doing the math.

_____

6. *Multiplying Decimals*

6.1 Estimating the Product of Decimal Numbers

Walt worked 12.7 hours last week. He gets $9.25 per hour. About how much did he earn last week?

This problem asks for an estimate of Walt's earnings

To find the exact solution, you multiply 12.7 × 9.25.

To find an estimate of this product, first round 12.7 and 9.25 to the nearest whole numbers:

12.7 rounds to 13

9.25 rounds to 9

Then multiply:

$$
\begin{array}{r}
13 \\
\times\ 9 \\
\hline
117
\end{array}
$$

Walt earned about $117 last week.

- -

HOW TO *estimate the product of two decimal numbers:*

1. Round each decimal number to the nearest whole number.

2. If one of the numbers is a whole number, leave it the way it is.

3. Multiply the rounded numbers—the product is the estimate.

EXAMPLE 1

Estimate the product of 45.58 × 19.9

Round 45.58 to the nearest whole number: 45.58 ——> 46

Round 19.9 to the nearest whole number: 19.9 ——> 20

Multiply the rounded numbers:

$$\begin{array}{r} 46 \\ \times\ 20 \\ \hline 920 \end{array}$$

EXAMPLE 2

Estimate the product of 73 × 15.36

73 is a whole number. Don't change it.

Round 15.36 to the nearest whole number: 15.36 ——> 15

Multiply the whole numbers:

$$\begin{array}{r} 73 \\ \times\ 15 \\ \hline 365 \\ 730 \\ \hline 1095 \end{array}$$

Exercises with Hints

Round these numbers to the nearest whole number. *(Hint: Use the number in the tenths place to decide whether you round up or down.)*

1. 2.6 _____

2. 72.5 _____

3. 200.4 _____

4. 8.52 _____

Estimate the product of the whole number and the decimal number.
(Hint: Round the decimal number only.)

5. 43 × 79.9 = _____

6. 72.5 × 30 = _____

7. 5.28 × 54 = _____

Estimate the product of the two decimal numbers. *(Hint: Round both decimal numbers to the nearest whole number.)*

8. 4.43 × 18.5 = _____

9. 25.38 × 8.81 = _____

10. 49.62 × 3.37 = _____

Solve.

11. Janus drank seven bottles of apple juice one week. Each bottle contains 6.7 ounces of juice. About how much juice did Janus drink? *(Hint: Round the decimal number before you multiply.)*

_____

12. Nora bought 3.25 pounds of cheese at $4.67 for each pound. About how much did she pay altogether? *(Hint: Round both decimal numbers before you multiply.)*

_____

Exercises on Your Own _____

Round to the nearest whole number.

1. 44.5 _____

2. 7.09 _____

3. 805.49 _____

4. 19.801 _____

Estimate the products.

5. 6.8 × 2.33 = _____

6. 189.5 × 40 = _____

7. 33.27 × 19.3 = _____

8. 35 × 2.7 = _____

9. 257 × 79.5 = _____

10. 95.1 × 4.002 = _____

Solve.

11. Nat drives the same route to work and back every day. The distance is 17.5 miles. About how many miles does he drive to and from work each week? (Assume that he works five days a week.)

_____

12. Clara bought a 16.54 pound turkey at $3.28 a pound. About how much did she pay altogether?

_____

99

6.2 Multiplying Whole Numbers by Decimals—Using Estimating to Place the Decimal Point

Ruth brought nine packages to the post office. Each package weighed 14.7 pounds. How much did they weigh altogether?

To solve the problem, multiply 14.7 × 9

Use estimation to place the decimal point in the product.

First, round 14.7 to the nearest whole number: 14.7 ——> 15

Then, estimate the product:

$$
\begin{array}{r}
15 \\
\times\ 9 \\
\hline
135
\end{array} \quad \longleftarrow \textit{estimate}
$$

Now do the exact multiplication. Multiply the decimal 14.7 and the whole number 9. For now, leave out the decimal points:

$$
\begin{array}{r}
147 \\
\times\ 9 \\
\hline
1323
\end{array}
$$

Now use the estimate to place the decimal point in the product. The estimate of 135 is close to 132.3

The packages weighed 132.3 pounds altogether.

- -

HOW TO *multiply whole numbers by decimals:*

1. Estimate the product of the whole number and decimal.
2. Multiply the whole number and decimal without the decimal point.
3. Use your estimate from Step 1 to locate where the decimal point belongs in the product.
4. Write the decimal point.

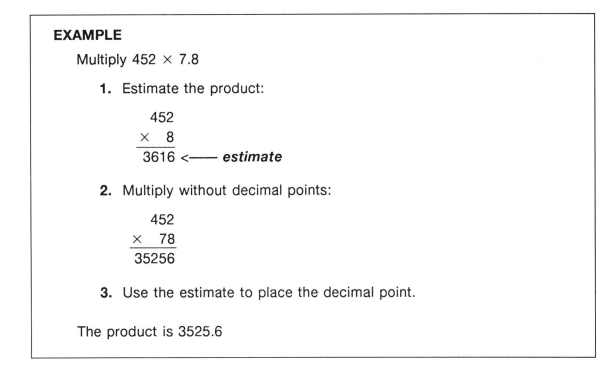

EXAMPLE

Multiply 452 × 7.8

1. Estimate the product:

$$
\begin{array}{r}
452 \\
\times\ \ 8 \\
\hline
3616 \\
\end{array}
$$
<—— **estimate**

2. Multiply without decimal points:

$$
\begin{array}{r}
452 \\
\times\ \ 78 \\
\hline
35256 \\
\end{array}
$$

3. Use the estimate to place the decimal point.

The product is 3525.6

Exercises with Hints

Round these numbers to the nearest whole number.
(Hint: Use the number in the tenths place to round.)

1. 50.4 _____

2. 28.57 _____

3. 178.38 _____

4. 59.9 _____

Estimate the product.
(Hint: Round the decimal number to the nearest whole number before multiplying.)

5. 6.7 × 38 = _____

6. 29.3 × 80 = _____

7. 3 × 84.5 = _____

Find the product.
(Hint: Use the estimates in Questions 5-7 to place the decimal points in the products.)

8. 6.7 × 38 = _____

9. 29.3 × 80 = _____

10. 3 × 84.5 = _____

Solve.

11. The packages that Gregg mails each month to his clients costs $3.65 per package in postage. Gregg mails 325 packages each month. How much does the monthly mailing cost?
(Hint: Use an estimate of the product to locate the decimal point in the answer.)

_____

12. Luanne works 6.85 hours each day according to the printout in the bookkeeping department of her company. How many hours did she work last month when she worked 22 days?

_____

Exercises on Your Own _____

Estimate the product.

1. 7.7 × 38 = _____

2. 190 × 2.3 = _____

3. 19.5 × 83 = _____

Place the decimal point in the products.

4. 35.2 × 8 = 2816

5. 305.4 × 18 = 54972

6. 22.1 × 87 = 19227

Find the product.

7. 33.8 × 20 = _____

8. 49.6 × 28 = _____

9. 206.5 × 42 = _____

10. 4.9 × 17 = _____

11. 300 × 48.5 = _____

12. 222 × 9.9 = _____

Solve.

13. Billie's talk show lasts 3.7 hours each day. If the show is on 6 days a week, what is the total number of hours that the show is on the air each week ?

_____

14. Dan works 48 hours each week and earns $12.78 per hour. How much does he earn each week?

_____

15. Coretta drives 26.4 miles each day to work and back. How many miles did she drive last month, when she made 24 round trips?

_____

6.3 Multiplying Decimals by 10, 100, and 1000

Molly lives in a town whose area is 6.4 square miles.

Doug lives in a city that is 100 times the area of Molly's town.

What is the area of Doug's city?

To find the answer, multiply 6.4 × 100.

Here's how you learned to multiply by a decimal in the last lesson:

First, estimate the product:

$$\begin{array}{r} 100 \\ \times\ \ 6 \\ \hline 600 \end{array}$$

Then multiply with the decimal:

$$\begin{array}{r} 100 \\ \times\ 6.4 \\ \hline 6400 \end{array}$$

Use the estimate to place the decimal point in the product: 640.0

The area of Doug's city is 640 square miles.

- -

A faster way to multiply 6.4 × 100 is to move the decimal point two places to the right.

6.4 × 100 = 6.40. or 640

103

HOW TO *multiply a decimal by 10, 100, and 1000:*

GENERAL RULE: Move the decimal point to the right the same number of places as the number of zeros:

1. To multiply by 10, move the decimal point 1 place to the right.
2. To multiply by 100, move the decimal point 2 places to the right.
3. To multiply by 1000, move the decimal point 3 places to the right.

EXAMPLE 1

Multiply 3.457×100

You are multiplying by **100**. Move the decimal point **two** places to the right:

$$3.457 \longrightarrow 3.45\underset{\curvearrowright}{.}7 = 345.7$$

EXAMPLE 2

Multiply 169.4×10

You are multiplying by **10**. Move the decimal point **one** place to the right:

$$169.4 \longrightarrow 169.4\underset{\curvearrowright}{.} = 1694$$

EXAMPLE 3

Multiply 2.09×1000

You are multiplying by **1000**. Move the decimal point **three** places to the right.

$$2.09 \longrightarrow 2.090\underset{\curvearrowright}{.} \longleftarrow \text{(Write a zero for the extra place)} = 2090$$

Exercises with Hints

How many places would you move the decimal point to the right when you multiply by these numbers?
(Hint: Count the number of zeros.)

1. 100 _____

2. 1000 _____

3. 10 _____

How many zeros do you need to write for the extra places? Answers can be 0, 1, or 2. *(Hint: See Example 3. You need extra places if there aren't enough digits.)*

4. $4.5 \times 100 =$ _____

5. $3.2 \times 1000 =$ _____

6. $17.984 \times 10 =$ _____

Multiply.
(Hint: Move the decimal point according to the number of zeros.)

7. 3.5 × 10 = _____

8. 17.32 × 10 = _____

9. 187.541 × 10 = _____

10. 8.13 × 100 = _____

11. 10.451 × 100 = _____

12. 1.8 × 100 = _____

13. 56.218 × 1000 = _____

14. 8.41 × 1000 = _____

15. 103.9 × 1000 = _____

16. 0.56 × 10 = _____

17. 0.04 × 100 = _____

18. 0.05 × 1000 = _____

Solve.

19. In Diego's city, the tallest building is 10 times the height of the post office. The post office is 35.8 feet high. How high is the tallest building?
(Hint: Count the number of zeros and move the decimal point that many places.)

_____

20. Shika makes $9.45 every hour. How much will she earn in 1000 hours?
(Hint: Follow the "How to" rule)

_____

Exercises on Your Own _____

How many places would you move the decimal point to the right when you multiply by these numbers?

1. 10,000 _____

2. 1,000,000 _____

3. 100,000 _____

Answer **T (true)** or **F (false)**.

4. 4.67 × 1000 = 4670 _____

5. 107.361 × 10 = 10736.1 _____

6. 400.8 × 1000 = 4008 _____

7. 1.723 × 100 = 1723 _____

Multiply.

8. 4.91 × 100 = _____

9. 39.6 × 1000 = _____

10. 1.402 × 10 = _____

11. 104.5 × 100 = _____

12. 5.555 × 100 = _____

13. 8.71 × 1000 = _____

14. 0.417 × 1000 = _____

15. 0.3 × 100 = _____

Solve.

16. Benny earned $12.65 per hour. How much money does he make after 100 hours of work?

_____

17. The smallest container in an industrial chemistry lab has a capacity of 0.25 liters. The largest container holds 1000 times more. What is the capacity of the largest container?

_____

6.4 *Multiplying Decimals by Decimals*

Dwight worked 37.4 hours last week. He earns $14.72 per hour. How much did he earn last week?

To solve this problem, multiply 14.72 × 37.4.

First, estimate the product of the two decimals.

Round 14.72 to the nearest whole number: 14.72 ——> 15

Round 37.4 to the nearest whole number: 37.4 ——> 37

Multiply the rounded numbers:

```
        15
     ×  37
      ─────
       105
       450
      ─────
       555  <—— estimated product
```

Next, do the complete multiplication.

Multiply the two decimals without their decimal points:

```
        1472
     ×   374
     ───────
        5888
      103040
      441600
      ───────
      550528  <—— product without decimal point
```

Use the estimate of 555 to write the decimal point in the product. Start from the right, and write a point 3 places from the right.

550528 ——> 550.528

Then round it to the nearest hundredth (that is, to the nearest cent.)

550.528 ——> 550.53

Dwight earned $550.53 last week.

Here's a faster way to find out where to write the decimal point.

HOW TO *place the decimal point in the product of two decimals:*

---

1. Multiply the two decimal numbers without their decimal points.

2. Count the number of decimal places to the right of the decimal point in each number.

3. Add these two amounts.

4. Use this sum to mark off the decimal places of the product. Start from the right and move left.

5. Write the decimal point.

EXAMPLE 1

Multiply 14.2 × 2.9

$$
\begin{array}{r}
14.2 \\
\times\ 2.9 \\
\hline
4118
\end{array}
$$

14.2 ←—— 1 decimal place after the decimal point
× 2.9 ←—— + 1 decimal place
4118 ←—— 2 decimal places

Mark off 2 decimal places from the right, moving left: 41.18.

The product is 41.18.

EXAMPLE 2

Multiply 2.363 × 7.5

2.363 ←—— 3 decimal places
× 7.5 ←—— + 1 decimal place
177225 ←—— 4 decimal places

Mark off 4 decimal places from the right, moving left: 17.7225.

The product is 17.7225.

Exercises with Hints

For each decimal, how many decimal places are there to the right of the decimal point?
(Hint: Start at the decimal point.)

1. 4.2 _____

2. 902.43 _____

3. 70.285 _____

4. 2094.1 _____

How many decimal places do you need to mark off in the product?
(Hint: Add the decimal places for each decimal number.)

5. 2.376 × 1.2 = _____

6. 40.05 × 3.75 = _____

7. 490 × 6.98 = _____

8. 1000.01 × 5.287 = _____

Mark the decimal point in the product.
(Hint: Add decimal places . . . Start from the right when you mark decimal places in the product.)

9.
$$\begin{array}{r} 3.41 \\ \times\ 1.9 \\ \hline 6479 \end{array}$$

10.
$$\begin{array}{r} 72.48 \\ \times\ 6.027 \\ \hline 43683696 \end{array}$$

11.
$$\begin{array}{r} 306.9 \\ \times\ 43.8 \\ \hline 1344222 \end{array}$$

Find the product.
(Hint: Place the number with the greater number of digits on top...multiply both numbers without the decimal points...mark the decimal point in the product.)

12.
$$\begin{array}{r} 6.3 \\ \times\ 7.04 \end{array}$$

13.
$$\begin{array}{r} 8.5 \\ \times\ 3.903 \end{array}$$

14.
$$\begin{array}{r} 7.2 \\ \times\ 1.8 \end{array}$$

Solve.

15. The length of a conference room is 6.9 meters and its width is 4.7 meters. What is the area of the room?
(Hint: Count the total number of decimal places and mark the decimal point in the product.)

_____

16. Rosa earns $95.45 each day. The computer made a mistake and paid her for 42.4 days last month. How much money did she earn, according to the computer?

_____

Exercises on Your Own

For each decimal number, how many places are there to the right of the decimal point?

1. 1704.403 _____

2. 4.444 _____

3. 15.8295 _____

4. 3.3 _____

How many decimal places do you need to mark off in the product?

5. 14.994 × 1.57 = _____

6. 300.4 × 8 = _____

7. 6.004 × 4.1 = _____

8. 6901.3 × 4991.7 = _____

Mark the decimal point in the product.

9.
$$\begin{array}{r} 45.78 \\ \times\ 5.8 \\ \hline 265524 \end{array}$$

10.
$$\begin{array}{r} 209.513 \\ \times\ 4.2 \\ \hline 8799546 \end{array}$$

11.
$$\begin{array}{r} 309.2 \\ \times\ 88.4 \\ \hline 2733328 \end{array}$$

Find the product and round to the nearest cent.

12. 4.6 × $35.43 _____

13. 9.4 × $3.48 _____

Find the product.

14.
$$\begin{array}{r} 42.9 \\ \times\ 1.6 \\ \hline \end{array}$$

15.
$$\begin{array}{r} 8.2 \\ \times\ 2.4 \\ \hline \end{array}$$

16.
$$\begin{array}{r} 7.034 \\ \times\ 1.8 \\ \hline \end{array}$$

Solve.

17. Todd found out that it costs $3.76 per pound to ship his package express. If the package weighs 7.4 pounds, what is the cost of shipping?

_____

18. A poster that Jill's company designed is 1.2 meters high and 0.8 meter wide. What is the area of the poster?

_____

19. Rosa earns $95.45 each day. The computer finally got it right and paid her for 21.2 days last month. How much money did she earn?

_____

6.5 Multiplying Decimals: Zeros in the Product

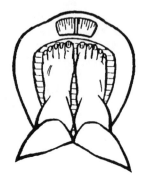

Carmen is on a diet. She lost 0.08 kilograms each day for 10 days.

Frank lost 0.7 of the amount that Carmen lost.

How much did Frank lose each day?

To find the answer, multiply: 0.7×0.08

Multiply without the decimal points: $8 \times 7 = 56$

Then add the number of decimal places of the two decimals:

$$
\begin{array}{rl}
.7 \longleftarrow & \text{1 decimal place} \\
\times \;\; 0.08 \longleftarrow & + \quad \text{2 decimal places} \\
\hline
56 \longleftarrow & \text{needs 3 decimal places, but has only 2}
\end{array}
$$

Place a zero to the left of 56 and write a decimal point:

$$0.056$$

Now your answer has 3 decimal places.

Frank lost 0.056 kilograms.

- -

WHEN TO *place zeros in the product of two decimals:*

1. Multiply the two decimals without the decimal points.
2. Find the number of decimal places needed for the product.
3. If the product does not have enough places, write zeros to the left of the product.
4. Write the decimal point in the product.

EXAMPLE 1

Multiply 0.3 × 0.004 = ?

    1. Multiply without the decimal points: 3 × 4 = 12

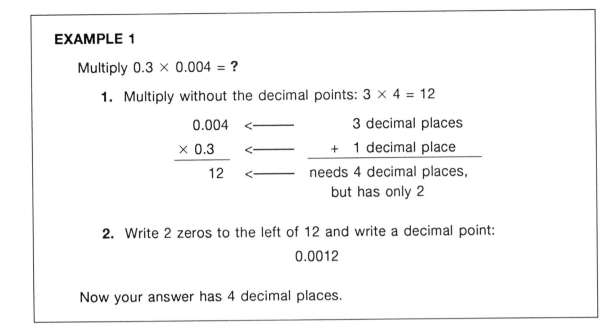

                 0.004   <——   3 decimal places

             × 0.3   <——   + 1 decimal place

                12   <—— needs 4 decimal places,
                                             but has only 2

    2. Write 2 zeros to the left of 12 and write a decimal point:

                          0.0012

Now your answer has 4 decimal places.

EXAMPLE 2

Multiply 0.09 × 0.07 = ?

    1. Multiply without the decimal points: 9 × 7 = 63

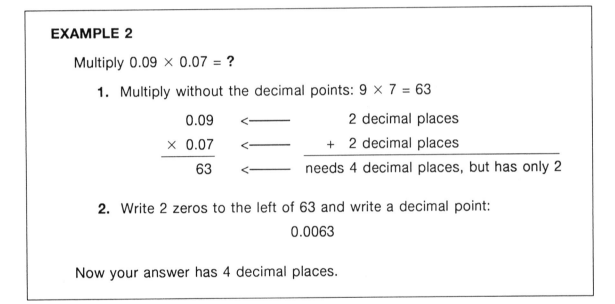

               0.09   <——   2 decimal places

             × 0.07   <—— + 2 decimal places

               63   <—— needs 4 decimal places, but has only 2

    2. Write 2 zeros to the left of 63 and write a decimal point:

                          0.0063

Now your answer has 4 decimal places.

Exercises with Hints

How many decimal places are there to the right of the decimal point?
(Hint: Count from the decimal point.)

1. 0.34 _____

2. 0.006 _____

3. 0.0007 _____

4. 9001.2 _____

What is the product when you multiply without the decimal points.
(Hint: First, write the decimal numbers without the decimal points.)

5. 0.02 × 0.08 = _____

6. 0.007 × 0.006 = _____

7. 0.05 × 0.5 = _____

How many decimal places are there in the product? Do not multiply.
(Hint: Add the decimal places of each decimal.)

8. 2.007 × 4.03 = _____

9. 0.06 × 0.03 = _____

10. 0.002 × 0.8 = _____

Multiply.
(Hint: Write zeros in the product to add decimal places.)

11. 0.2 × 0.006 = _____

12. 0.007 × 0.7 = _____

13. 0.005 × 0.003 = _____

Multiply.
(Hint: Write the longer number on top.)

14. 4.5 × 3.081 = _____

15. 2.7 × 4.251 = _____

Solve.

16. The area of the computer chip that Gladys' company makes is 0.08 cm^2 (0.08 square centimeters). Gladys wants the area of the new chip to be 0.7 of the present area. What will be the area of the new chip?
(Hint: Write zeros in the product to add decimal places.)

_____

Exercises on Your Own

How many decimal places are there to the right of the decimal point?

1. 4.891 _____

2. 0.02 _____

3. 0.0001 _____

4. 4001.089 _____

What is the product when you multiply without the decimal points?

5. $0.004 \times 0.09 =$ _____

6. $0.03 \times 0.05 =$ _____

7. $0.001 \times 0.009 =$ _____

How many decimal places are there in the product? Do not multiply.

8. $0.176 \times 0.001 =$ _____

9. $208.06 \times 0.05 =$ _____

10. $0.008 \times 0.8 =$ _____

Multiply.

11. $1.2 \times 0.004 =$ _____

12. $0.09 \times 0.05 =$ _____

13. $0.7 \times 0.003 =$ _____

14. $2.43 \times 8.9 =$ _____

15. $7.002 \times 0.1 =$ _____

16. $0.006 \times 4.2 =$ _____

17. $8.3 \times 4.003 =$ _____

18. $3.4 \times 7.913 =$ _____

19. $0.7 \times 2.001 =$ _____

20. $\$1.27 \times 7 =$ _____

21. $\$2.07 \times 2.3 =$ _____

22. $0.05 \times 0.35 =$ _____

Solve.

23. Paula calculated that it costs $0.02 for each photocopy made in her office. As manager, she wants to reduce the cost to 0.7 of the present cost. What will the new cost be?

_____

6.6 Review

Estimate the products. Round to the nearest whole number and multiply.

1. $8.6 \times 7.3 =$ _____

2. $199.7 \times 39.6 =$ _____

3. $66 \times 9.9 =$ _____

4. $72.6 \times 8.7. =$ _____

5. $3.4 \times 84.539 =$ _____

Find the products.

6. $42.7 \times 34 =$ _____

7. $79.5 \times 75 =$ _____

8. $208.6 \times 8 =$ _____

9. $3.8 \times 16 =$ _____

10. $200 \times 78.4 =$ _____

How many places would you move the decimal point to the right when you multiply by these numbers?

11. 1000 _____

12. 10,000 _____

13. 1,000,000 _____

Multiply.

14. $\$7.63 \times 1000 =$ _____

15. $285.294 \times 10 =$ _____

16. $700.8 \times 1000 =$ _____

17. $9.237 \times 100 =$ _____

18. $0.763 \times 10 =$ _____

19. $\$5.92 \times 1000 =$ _____

20. $0.004 \times 100 =$ _____

Mark the decimal point in the product.

21.
$$\begin{array}{r} 32.984 \\ \times\ 4.67 \\ \hline 15403528 \end{array}$$

22.
$$\begin{array}{r} \$5.98 \\ \times\ 2.72 \\ \hline \$162656 \end{array}$$

Find the product.

23.
$$\begin{array}{r} 8.7 \\ \times\ \$4.06 \\ \hline \end{array}$$

24.
$$\begin{array}{r} \$25.37 \\ \times\ 5.21 \\ \hline \end{array}$$

25.
$$\begin{array}{r} 9.709 \\ \times\ 26.44 \\ \hline \end{array}$$

Multiply.

26. $2.1 \times 0.002 =$ _____

27. $0.07 \times 0.06 =$ _____

28. $0.9 \times 0.005 =$ _____

29. $\$3.65 \times 4.2 =$ _____

30. $2.007 \times 0.3 =$ _____

31. $0.003 \times 6.7 =$ _____

32. $200.5 \times 3.008 =$ _____

33. $7.3 \times 1.205 =$ _____

34. $0.4 \times 7.005 =$ _____

35. $1.85 × 5 = _____

36. $6.36 × 4.1 = _____

37. 0.07 × 0.28 = _____

Solve.

38. Marty bought 12 pairs of basketball shoes for the team. Each pair cost $67.95. Estimate the total cost of the shoes.

_____

39. Each bottle of glue contains 7.8 ounces. Estimate how many ounces of glue there are in 15 bottles.

_____

40. Jesse begins each day by walking around the park in his neighborhood, 3.1 miles long. Estimate how far Jesse walks in 365 days.

_____

41. Each box of computer paper costs $45.37. How much do 75 boxes cost?

_____

42. A large bottle of soda costs $1.65. How much do 24 bottles cost?

_____

43. Kareem sold 75 ties last month. Each tie sells for $12.75. What was Kareem's income from selling ties?

_____

44. Hilda saves $56 each week from her pay check. How much will she save in 100 weeks?

_____

45. Yolanda said that each layer of cardboard measures 0.09 inch. How thick would 10 layers of cardboard be?

_____

46. Masako estimates that in 10 years the rate of growth of the population in his community will be 1000 times the present rate, which is 0.6 per cent. What will the population growth rate be?

_____

47. Todd built an addition to his house. It was 14.5 feet by 17.8 feet. What is the area of the addition to the house?

_____

48. Flora started a new job last month. She gets paid $14.75 an hour. She works 36.25 hours each week. How much does she make each week?

_____

49. Norma wants to reduce the cost of each phone call to 0.7 of its present cost. The average cost now is $0.13. What will be the new average cost? (Round to the nearest cent.)

_____

50. Mitchell estimates that by switching phone companies, his company saved $0.06 per phone call last year. He would like to save 0.7 more this year. How much money does he want to save? (Round to the nearest cent.)

_____

7. *Dividing Decimals*

7.1 Dividing Decimals by Whole Numbers

Ron, Jan, and Carl split their bill for lunch. It was $25.56, including tax and tip.

How much did each person have to pay?

To find the answer divide: $25.56 ÷ 3 = ?

First, set up the division problem in the usual way:

<——— *quotient (the answer) goes here*

divisor ——> 3) 25.56 <——— *dividend*

Write a decimal point in the place where the quotient (the answer) will go, right above the decimal point of the dividend 25.56

$$3 \overline{)\ 25.56}$$

Divide the same way that you would with whole numbers.

```
        8.52   <——— quotient (the answer)
   3 ) 25.56
      − 24
        1 5
      − 1 5
        0 6
      −   6
          0   <——— remainder
```

They each paid $8.52 for lunch.

HOW TO *divide a decimal by a whole number:*

> *1.* Write a decimal point in the quotient directly above the decimal point of the dividend.
>
> *2.* Divide as if both numbers were whole numbers.
>
> *3.* Check to see that the quotient makes sense.

EXAMPLE

Divide: 5194.35 ÷ 63 = **?**

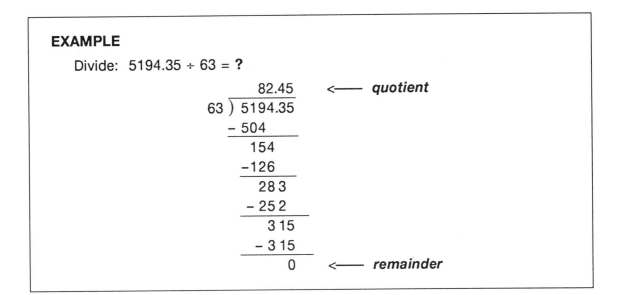

Exercises with Hints

Place a check mark after the whole numbers.

(Hint: Whole numbers are: 1, 2, 3, and so forth. Fractions and mixed decimals are not whole numbers.)

1. 45.8 _____

2. 7,239 _____

3. $\frac{3}{4}$ _____

4. 5 _____

Place a check mark after the examples that show a mixed decimal divided by a whole number.

(Hint: Make sure you read the division sign ÷ as "divided by.")

5. 389 ÷ 2.3 _____

6. 32.7 ÷ 2 _____

7. 451 ÷ 34 _____

Write the decimal point in each quotient.
(Hint: Place the decimal point directly above the decimal point in the dividend.)

$$\begin{array}{r} 17\,4 \\ 8)\overline{139.2} \end{array}$$

8.

$$\begin{array}{r} 20\,45 \\ 49\,)\overline{1002.05} \end{array}$$

9.

Divide.
(Hint: First place the decimal point. Then divide.)

10. $342.36 \div 6 =$ _____

11. $1005.42 \div 26 =$ _____

Solve.

12. Silva and his three friends spent $85.84 on bicycle parts. They split the costs. How much did each of them pay?
(Hint: First write the decimal point in the quotient. Then divide.)

_____

13. Luisa receives the same amount of salary each week. After eight weeks she received $2005.76. How much does she receive each week?

_____

Exercises on Your Own

Place a check mark after the whole numbers.

1. 437 _____

2. 14.6 _____

3. 200,098 _____

4. 128.009 _____

Place a check mark after the examples that show a decimal divided by a whole number.

5. $33.61 \div 2.4$ _____

6. $502.38 \div 6$ _____

7. $3.2 \div 9$ _____

Write the decimal point in each quotient.

$$\begin{array}{r} 85\,25 \\ 17\,)\overline{1449.25} \end{array}$$

8.

$$\begin{array}{r} 1\,357 \\ 85\,)\overline{115.345} \end{array}$$

9.

Divide.

10. $380.1 \div 7 =$ _____

11. $1606.54 \div 13 =$ _____

12. $785.16 \div 9 =$ _____

13. $753.27 \div 21 =$ _____

Solve.

14. Jon spent $869.40 for 12 pairs of running shoes for the track team. Each pair cost the same amount. How much did each pair cost?

_____

15. Joe needs to divide a copper pipe into five equal parts. The pipe is 239.05 cm long. How long will each part be?

_____

7.2 *Dividing Decimals by Whole Numbers: Zeros in the Dividend*

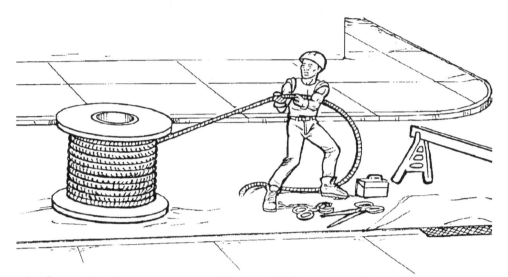

Seiji works for a telephone company. He has 36.4 meters of telephone cable. He cut the cable into 8 equal parts. How long was each part?

To find the answer, divide: 36.4 ÷ 8 = **?**

- Set up the problem in the usual way:

<————— **quotient (the answer) goes here**

divisor ———> 8) 36.4 <——— **dividend**

- Write a decimal point in the place where the quotient will go, right above the decimal point of 36.4.

$$8) \overline{36.4}$$

- Divide the same way you would with whole numbers.

```
      4.5
 8 ) 36.4
    -32
      4 4
     -4 0
        4      <——— remainder
```

So far, this is like the problem in the Lesson 7.1—with one difference.

There is a **remainder** of 4.

- To complete the division, place a zero in the hundredths place of the dividend and continue dividing:

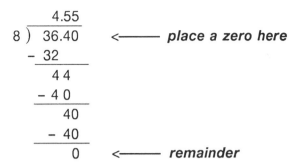

```
        4.55
  8 ) 36.40          <——— place a zero here
     - 32
     ─────
       4 4
      - 4 0
      ─────
        40
      - 40
      ─────
         0           <——— remainder
```

Seiji has eight pieces of cable, each 4.55 meters long.

- -

HOW TO *complete a division example by placing zeros to the right of the decimal:*

---

1. Write a decimal point in the quotient above the decimal point of the dividend.

2. Divide as if both numbers were whole numbers.

3. If there is a remainder, place one or more zeros to the right of the decimal.

4. Continue to divide until the remainder is 0.

EXAMPLE 1

Divide: 471.6 ÷ 24 = **?**

```
          19.65
   24 )471.60          <——— place a 0 here
      - 24
      ─────
        231
      - 216
      ─────
         15 6
       - 14 4
       ──────
          1 20
        - 1 20
        ──────
            0          <——— remainder
```

121

EXAMPLE 2

Divide: 918 ÷ 48 = ?

This is a case of a whole number divided by a whole number. But you follow the method outlined in this chapter.

```
        19. 125
48 ) 918.000          <———  write a decimal point and add zeros
   – 48                       until the remainder is 0
     438
   – 432
       6 0
     – 4 8
       1 20
       – 96
        240
      – 240
          0          <———  remainder
```

Exercises with Hints

Which examples show a decimal divided by a whole number?
(Hint: Remember—the number after the ÷ sign is the number you divide by.)

1. 23.47 ÷ 45 = ?

2. 400 ÷ 2.8 = ?

3. 4.002 ÷ 7 = ?

Divide.
(Hint: Place zeros to the right of the decimal point until the remainder is 0.)

4. 33.4 ÷ 8 = _____

5. 5 ÷ 8 = _____

6. 672 ÷15 = _____

7. 16.73 ÷ 14 = _____

8. 6.35 ÷ 25 = _____

9. 6.8 ÷ 8 = _____

Solve.

10. Yolanda wants to cut 60.3 meters of telephone cable into eight equal pieces. How long will each piece be?
(Hint: Place zeros to the right of the decimal point when you divide until the remainder is zero.)

_____

11. Marty decided to invest all of his savings—$4064. He invests an equal amount each month for 5 months. How much does he invest each month?

_____

Exercises on Your Own

Divide.

1. 7 ÷ 16 = _____

2. 1.19 ÷ 5 = _____

3. 78 ÷ 15 = _____

4. 18.34 ÷ 35 = _____

5. 42.3 ÷ 18 = _____

6. 38 ÷ 40 = _____

7. 2.6 ÷ 8 = _____

8. 50.7 ÷ 78 = _____

9. 9 ÷ 60 = _____

Solve.

10. John bought 3.6 pounds of beef to make hamburgers. He made 8 hamburgers, using the same amount of beef for each hamburger. How much beef did he use for each hamburger?

_____

11. Joyce and 11 classmates went on a trip that cost $591. If they split the cost of the trip, how much did each person pay?

_____

7.3 Dividing by 10, 100, and 1000

Joan mails 10 packages at the Post Office. Together the packages weigh 64.7 pounds. If all the packages weigh the same amount, how much does each package weigh?

To find the solution, divide: 64.7 ÷ 10 = **?**

```
          6.47
   10 )  64.70     <— place a zero in the hundredths place
      −  60
          4 7
       −  4 0
            70
          − 70
             0
```

Each package weighs 6.47 pounds.

When we divide 64.7 by 10, the quotient is 6.47.

A faster way to divide 64.7 by 10 is to move the decimal point one place to the left.

$$64.7 \div 10 = 6.4.7 \text{ or } 6.47$$

HOW TO divide a decimal by 10, 100, and 1000:

General rule: Move the decimal point to the left the same number of places as the number of zeros:

1. To divide by **10**, move the decimal point **one** place to the left.
2. To divide by **100**, move the decimal point **two** places to the left.
3. To divide by **1000**, move the decimal point **three** places to the left.

EXAMPLE 1

Divide 735.65 ÷ 100 = **?**

Since division is by **100**, move the decimal point **two** places to the left (See Rule 2, above):

735.65 ——> 7.35.65 = 7.3565

EXAMPLE 2

Divide 6.03 ÷10 = **?**

Since the division is by **10**, move the decimal point **one** place to the left (See Rule 1, above):

6.03 ——> 0.6.03 = 0.603

EXAMPLE 3

Divide 39.5 ÷ 1000 = **?**

Since the division is by **1000**, move the decimal point **three** places to the left (See Rule 3, above):

39.5 —> **0.**039.5 <— Write a zero to the left of the 3 for the extra
place = 0.0395

Exercises with Hints

How many places would you move the decimal point to the left when you divide by these numbers?
(Hint: Count the number of zeros.)

1. 100: ___ places

2. 1000: ___ places

3. 10: ___ places

4. 10,000: ___ places

How many zeros do you need to put in for extra places? Answers can be 0, 1, or 2.
(Hint: Remember that you move the decimal point to the left when you divide.)

5. $4.26 \div 1000$ _____

6. $9.72 \div 100$ _____

7. $73.6 \div 10$ _____

By what number did we divide the number on the left to get the quotient on the right?
(Hint: Count the number of places the decimal was moved.)

Number Started With	Divided By	Quotient
8. 39.6	_____	0.396
9. 4,981	_____	498.1
10. 6.023	_____	0.006023
11. 0.619	_____	0.00619
12. 12000	_____	120

(Hint: Remember that there is an "invisible" decimal point after every whole number.)

Divide.
(Hint: Count the number of zeros of the divisor.)

13. $67.3 \div 10 =$ _____

14. $673 \div 1000 =$ _____

15. $0.673 \div 1000 =$ _____

16. $6.73 \div 100 =$ _____

Solve.

17. Nick divided a piece of paper into 10 equal columns. The paper measures 20.5 centimeters wide. How wide is each column?
(Hint: Move the decimal point to the left.)

_____

Exercises on Your Own

How many places would you move the decimal point to the left when you divide by these numbers?

1. 1000: ____ places

2. 10: ____ places

3. 10,000: ____ places

4. 100,000: ____ places

Answer **T (true)** or **F (false)**:

5. When you divide by 100, the answer is less than the number you started with.

_____

6. When you multiply by 100, the answer is less than the number you started with.

_____

By what number did we divide the number on the left to get the quotient on the right?

	Number Started With	Divided By	Quotient
7.	5.87	_____	0.587
8.	0.912	_____	0.00912
9.	562.7	_____	0.5627
10.	14.7	_____	1.47
11.	3.891	_____	0.03891
12.	60,000	_____	600

Divide.

13. $6.7 \div 10 =$ _____

14. $6.7 \div 100 =$ _____

15. $6.7 \div 1000 =$ _____

16. $0.9 \div 10 =$ _____

17. $0.9 \div 100 =$ _____

18. $0.9 \div 1000 =$ _____

19. $406.35 \div 1000 =$ _____

20. $6.003 \div 100 =$ _____

Solve.

17. Kiri drove her car for 100 hours on a long trip last summer. She traveled 4380 miles. What was the average number of miles she traveled each hour?

_____

22. Carolee earned $26,982 over the last 10 months. She earns the same amount each month. How much did she earn each month?

_____

23. Leroy worked 100 hours on a special job. He earned $2,627. How much did he earn per hour?

_____

7.4 *Metric Measures: Multiplying and Dividing by 10, 100, and 1000*

Margo is measuring her staircase so that she can figure out the amount of carpet she needs. She says the staircase measures 564 centimeters. Write this length in meters.

To make the change from centimeters to meters, you need this table.

METRIC UNITS OF LENGTH

1 centimeter (cm) = 10 millimeters (mm)

1 meter (m) = 100 centimeters

1 kilometer (km) = 1000 meters

To change from a smaller unit to a larger unit, divide.

The centimeter is a smaller unit than the meter.

To change from centimeters to meters, divide by 100:

$$564 \div 100 = \textbf{?}$$

Since 564 is a whole number, we can write a decimal point to the right of the number:

$$564.$$

Dividing by 100 is the same as moving the decimal point two places to the left (see lesson 7.3):

$$564. \xrightarrow{\div \textbf{100}} 5.64. \text{ meters}$$

HOW TO *change from one metric unit to another:*

1. Decide if you are changing from a smaller unit to a larger unit, or from a larger unit to a smaller unit.

2. If you are changing from a smaller unit to a larger unit, **divide**.

3. If you are changing from a larger unit to a smaller unit, **multiply**.

4. If you are working with units of length, divide or multiply by the number in the table shown above. (If you are working with other kinds of units, like weight or volume, use one of the tables below.)

EXAMPLE 1

Change 6.476 kilograms to grams.

Use this table showing metric units of mass.

METRIC UNITS OF MASS

1 kilogram (kg) = 1000 grams (g)

1 gram = 1000 milligrams (mg)

Since the change is from a larger unit to a smaller unit, multiply by 1000:

Multiply 6.476 by 1000. Move the decimal point three decimal places to the right (see Lesson 6.3)

$$6.476 \xrightarrow{\times 1000} 6.476. = 6476 \text{ grams}$$

EXAMPLE 2

Change 4,982 milliliters to liters.

Use this table showing metric units of capacity.

METRIC UNITS OF CAPACITY

1 liter (l) = 1000 milliliters (ml)

Since the change is from a smaller unit to a larger unit, divide by 1000:

To divide 4,982 by 1000, move the decimal point three decimal places to the left:

$$4,982 \xrightarrow{\div 1000} 4.982. = 4.982 \text{ liters}$$

EXAMPLE 3

Change 35.69 centimeters to millimeters.

Use this table showing metric units of length.

<u>METRIC UNITS OF LENGTH</u>

1 centimeter = 10 millimeters

1 meter = 100 centimeters

1 kilometer = 1000 meters

Since we need to change from a larger unit to a smaller unit, multiply by 10:

Multiply 35.69 by 10 by moving the decimal point one decimal place to the right:

$$35.69 \xrightarrow{\times\ 10} 35.6.9 = 356.9 \text{ centimeters}$$

Exercises with Hints

Is the change from a smaller unit to a larger unit, or from a larger unit to a smaller unit? Check the correct choice after each problem (You don't have to make the change.)
(Hint: To help you with the following problems, use one of the three tables shown above.)

1. 3476 centimeters = ___ meters

    a. larger to smaller ___

    b. smaller to larger ___

2. 853 kilograms = ___ grams

    a. larger to smaller ___

    b. smaller to larger ___

3. 94,128 milliliters = ___ liters

    a. larger to smaller ___

    b. smaller to larger ___

4. 45.27 centimeters = ___ millimeters

    a. larger to smaller ___

    b. smaller to larger ___

5. 803.76 milligrams = ___ grams

    a. larger to smaller ___

    b. smaller to larger ___

6. 45.37 meters = ___ centimeters

    a. larger to smaller ___

    b. smaller to larger ___

7. 24 kilometers = ___ meters

    a. larger to smaller ___

    b. smaller to larger ___

8. 9.35 liters = _____ milliliters

    a. larger to smaller _____

    b. smaller to larger _____

Do you multiply or divide to find the missing measures? Mark the correct answers.
(Hint: Use the rules and the answers to Exercises 1-8.)

9. 3476 centimeters = _____ meters

    a. multiply _____

    b. divide _____

10. 853 kilograms = _____ grams

    a. multiply _____

    b. divide _____

11. 94,128 milliliters = _____ liters

    a. multiply _____

    b. divide _____

12. 45.27 centimeters = ___ millimeters

    a. multiply _____

    b. divide _____

13. 803.76 milligrams = _____ grams

    a. multiply _____

    b. divide _____

14. 45.37 meters = _____ centimeters

    a. multiply _____

    b. divide _____

15. 24 kilometers = _____ meters

    a. multiply _____

    b. divide _____

16. 9.35 liters = _____ milliliters

    a. multiply _____

    b. divide _____

Find the missing numbers.
(Hint: Use the answers of Exercises 9-16 and the tables in the Lesson.)

17. 3476 centimeters = _____ meters

18. 853 kilograms = _____ grams

19. 94,128 milliliters = _____ liters

20. 45.27 centimeters = ___ millimeters

21. 803.76 milligrams = _____ grams

22. 45.37 meters = _____ centimeters

23. 24 kilometers = _____ meters

24. 9.35 liters = _____ milliliters

Solve.

25. Dana walked 1.6 kilometers. Change this length to meters.
(Hint: Use the table in Example 3 showing metric units of length and the HOW TO section.)

    _____

26. Norma drank 450 milliliters of juice. Change this amount to liters.
(Hint: Use the table in Example 2 showing metric units of capacity and the HOW TO section.)

    _____

Exercises on Your Own

Do you multiply or divide to find the missing meaures? Mark the correct answers.

1. 8036 grams = _____ kilograms

    a. multiply _____

    b. divide _____

2. 783 milliliters = _____ liters

    a. multiply _____

    b. divide _____

3. 452 centimeters = _____ meters

    a. multiply _____

    b. divide _____

4. 3.76 liters = _____ milliliters

    a. multiply _____

    b. divide _____

5. 6.876 millimeters = _____ centimeters

    a. multiply _____

    b. divide _____

Find the missing measures.

6. 8036 grams = _____ kilograms

7. 783 milliliters = _____ liters

8. 452 centimeters = _____ meters

9. 3.76 liters = _____ milliliters

10. 6.876 millimeters = _____ centimeters

Solve.

11. There were 2.6 liters of water in the refrigerator. How many milliliters more than 2 liters is this?

    _____

12. Oreste weighs 62.7 kilograms. How many grams over 60 kilograms is this?

    _____

13. The length of a butterfly's wings in Harriet's collection is 32 millimeters. How many centimeters is that?

    _____

7.5 *Dividing Decimals by Tenths*

A can of paint holds 1.8 gallons of paint. Carmen needs 12.6 gallons of paint. How many cans does she need?

To find the answer, divide: 12.6 ÷ 1.8 = **?**

$$\text{\textbf{\textit{divisor}}} \longrightarrow 1.8 \,\overline{)\,12.6} \longleftarrow \text{\textbf{\textit{dividend}}}$$

Make the divisor a whole number. You can do that by multiplying both the divisor and dividend by 10:

$$1.8 \times 10 = 18$$
$$12.6 \times 10 = 126$$

Then divide:

$$\begin{array}{r} 7 \\ 18\,\overline{)\,126} \\ -126 \\ \hline 0 \end{array}$$

Carmen needs 7 cans of paint.

HOW TO *divide a decimal by a decimal in tenths:*

1. Make the divisor a whole number: multiply both the divisor and the dividend by 10.
2. Multiply by 10 the fast way: move the decimal points of both the dividend and divisor 1 place to the right.
3. Then divide, using the whole-number divisor.

EXAMPLE

Divide: 36.66 ÷ 4.7 = ?

Move the decimal points of the divisor and dividend 1 place to the right, and divide.

$$4.7 \longrightarrow 47$$

$$36.66 \longrightarrow 366.6$$

Then divide the usual way until you get a remainder of 0.

```
          7.8
   47) 366.6
      - 329
        37 6
      - 37 6
           0 <—— remainder
```

Exercises with Hints

Multiply each decimal by 10.
(Hint: How many places do you move the decimal point?)

1. 4.5 _____

2. 7.81 _____

3. 72.7 _____

4. 9.82 _____

Prepare these examples for division by rewriting each problem. Change the position of the decimal point in both the divisor and dividend. (Do not divide.)
(Hint: Move the decimal point the same number of places in both the divisor and the dividend.)

5. 34.7) 237.5 _____

6. 3.4) 31.8 _____

7. 45.9) 426.87 _____

Divide.
(Hint: The first step is to make the divisor into a whole number.)

8. 58.8 ÷ 4.9 = _____

9. 1357.2 ÷ 17.4 = _____

10. 109.48 ÷ 4.6 = _____

11. 527.52 ÷ 8.4 = _____

Solve.

12. Gordy designs and manufactures earrings. Each earring weighs 3.8 ounces. How many earrings does he have altogether if their total weight is 182.4 ounces?
(Hint: Move the decimal point the same number of places in the divisor and dividend.)

_____

Exercises on Your Own

Multiply each decimal by 10.

1. 5.2 _____

2. 5.92 _____

3. 7.02 _____

4. 611.2 _____

Prepare these examples for division by rewriting each problem. Change the position of the decimal point in both the divisor and dividend. (Do not divide.)

5. $3.7 \overline{)\ 18.5}$ _____

6. $4.8 \overline{)\ 43.68}$ _____

7. $8.2 \overline{)\ 54.94}$ _____

Divide.

8. $48.26 \div 3.8 =$ _____

9. $446.5 \div 9.4 =$ _____

10. $641.52 \div 32.4 =$ _____

11. $273.18 \div 47.1 =$ _____

Solve.

13. Dan brought several packages to the Post Office. Each package weighed 5.6 pounds. The total weight was 44.8 pounds. How many packages did Dan bring to the Post Office?

_____

14. Matthew has a rope that is 18.9 meters long. He wants to cut it into equal pieces 2.7 meters long. How many pieces will there be?

_____

15. Connie received a shipment of paper weighing 10.5 kilograms. How many boxes of paper are in the shipment if each box weighs 0.75 kilograms?

_____

7.6 Dividing Decimals by Hundredths and Thousandths

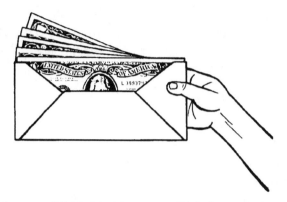

Alex's wages last week were $349.16. He earns $12.47 an hour. How many hours did he work last week?

To find the answer, divide: 349.16 ÷ 12.47 = **?**

$$12.47 \overline{)\ 349.16}$$

This is an example of a problem in which there are 2 decimal places in the divisor.

Make the divisor a whole number. You can do that by multiplying the divisor and dividend by 100:

$$12.47 \times 100 = 1247$$

$$349.16 \times 100 = 34916$$

Then divide:

```
              28
    1247 ) 34916
         - 2494
           9976
         - 9976
              0 <——— remainder
```

Alex worked 28 hours last week.

NOTE: In everyday life, difficult long division problems like the one above are often done with a calculator. It takes much longer to work them out by hand. However, you still should know the method of dividing by a decimal that is described above.

HOW TO divide a decimal by a decimal in hundredths or thousandths:

1. Make the divisor a whole number: multiply the divisor by 100 or 1000; multiply the dividend by 100 or 1000.

2. Multiply the fast way:

   If a divisor is a decimal in hundredths, move the decimal points of both the divisor and dividend 2 places to the right.

   If a divisor is a decimal in thousandths, move the decimal points of both the divisor and dividend 3 places to the right;

3. Then divide, using the whole number divisor.

EXAMPLE

Divide: 80.3 ÷ 9.125 = ?

This is an example of a problem in which there are 3 decimal places in the divisor.

Move the decimal points of the divisor and dividend 3 places to the right. Notice that to do this, you have to add 2 zeros to the dividend.

$$9.125 \longrightarrow 9125$$

$$80.3 \longrightarrow 80300 \longleftarrow \textit{Place 2 zeros to make 3 places}$$

Then divide:

```
                8.8  <—— quotient
        9125 ) 80300.0
             - 73000
               7300 0
             - 7300 0
                    0  <—— remainder
```

In most of the exercises that follow, you will work with setting up the problem, but you will not have to do the actual division. There are only a few problems in which you do have to divide, and the actual division will not be very hard.

Exercises with Hints

How many decimal places do we have to move the decimal point to make these numbers into whole numbers?
(Hint: Possible answers: 1, 2, 3, or 4 places)

1. 4.507 _____

2. 3017.4 _____

3. 400.06 _____

4. 71.0704 _____

Prepare these examples for division by rewriting each problem. Change the position of the decimal point in both the divisor and dividend. (Do not divide.)
(Hint: Move the decimal point the same number of places in both the divisor and the dividend. Add zeros to the dividend if you have to.)

5. $7.28 \overline{)60.1506}$ _____

6. $14.941 \overline{)65.2}$ _____

7. $3.061 \overline{)8.8}$ _____

Divide.
(Hint: The answer in each case consists of the numeral 2 and one or more zeros. Your main job is to find where to place the zeros and the decimal point in the quotient.)

8. 23 ÷ 1.15 = _____

9. 800.8 ÷ 4.004 = _____

10. 622.6 ÷ 3.113 = _____

Solve.

11. Daryl earns $8.45 per hour when he works weekends. He earned $143.65 over the last month. How many hours did he work?
(Hint: First, move the decimal point the same number of places in both the divisor and the dividend.)

_____

Exercises on Your Own

How many decimal places do we have to move the decimal point to make these numbers into whole numbers?

1. 9.03 _____

2. 13.827 _____

3. 62.0639 _____

4. 300.007 _____

Prepare these examples for division by making each divisor a whole number. Do not divide.

5. $3.517 \overline{)\ 13.761}$ _____

6. $17.04 \overline{)\ 90.4513}$ _____

7. $6.307 \overline{)\ 34.2}$ _____

Divide.

8. $2.68 \div 0.134 =$ _____

9. $1068 \div 5.34 =$ _____

10. $25 \div 1.25 =$ _____

Solve.

12. Joyce earned $256 last week. She gets $12.80 per hour. How many hours did she work?

_____

13. Erika placed stamps on a group of packages that had a total weight of 85 pounds. Each package weighed 2.5 pounds. How many packages did Erika place stamps on?

_____

14. A pill in a pill bottle weighs 2.2 grams. The entire bottle of pills (not counting the bottle) weighs 143 grams. How many pills are in the bottle?

_____

7.7 Dividing Decimals by Decimals: Rounding Quotients

Tarantella's Grocery bought 38.9 pounds of mozzarella cheese last month. Mr. Tarantella paid $148.50 for the cheese.

What is the average price Mr. Tarantella paid for each pound?

To find the average price, divide: 148.50 ÷ 38.9 = **?**

$$38.9 \overline{)\ 148.50}$$

If you have a calculator, use it to find the quotient.

On the calculator: 148.50 ÷ 38.9 = 3.8174807

Since we are dealing with money, we need to round the quotient to the nearest cent, which is the same as rounding to the nearest hundredth.

Look at the number in the thousandths place. It is a 7. The number 7 is greater than 5, so you round the number in the hundredths place up from 1 to 2.

The average price of a pound of cheese is $3.82.

HOW TO round quotients:

1. Decide in advance the number of decimal places you need to round to make sense for the quotient.

—If the answer is dollars and cents, you round to the nearest hundredth (2 decimal places).

2. Divide the long way or use a calculator.

3. Round the quotient to the nearest place that makes sense for the answer.

—If you are rounding to the nearest cent, look at the thousandths place (the third decimal place). If it is 5 or greater, round the hundredths place up.

EXAMPLE 1

$234.6 \div 5.9 = ?$ Round the quotient to the nearest hundredth.

Divide by calculator:

$234.6 \div 5.9 = 39.762712$

Rounded to the nearest hundredth = 39.76

EXAMPLE 2

$67.2 \div 4.5 = ?$ Round the quotient to the nearest tenth.

Divide the long way:

Move the decimal points of the divisor and dividend 1 place to the right:

$$4.5 \longrightarrow 45$$

$$67.2 \longrightarrow 672$$

Divide until the quotient shows the hundredth place.

```
         14.93          <——  quotient only as far as
    45) 672.00                hundredth place
       - 45
         222
       - 180
          42 0
        - 40 5
           1 50
         - 1 35
             15
```

14.93 rounded to the nearest tenth is 14.9.

141

Exercises with Hints

Round each number to the nearest tenth.

(Hint: The tenth place is 1 place to the right of the decimal point. But remember, you need to get a number for the hundredths place before you can decide whether to round up or round down. If the hundredths place is 5 or greater, you round up in the tenths place.)

1. 5.28 _____

2. 751.883 _____

3. 601.55 _____

Round to the nearest hundredth.
(Hint: The hundredth place is 2 places to the right of the decimal point. But you need 3 places to round to the nearest hundredth)

4. 8.267 _____

5. 2091.752 _____

6. 4.8952 _____

Round to the nearest thousandth.
(Hint: The thousandth place is 3 places to the right of the decimal point.)

7. 34.0073 _____

8. 100.3456 _____

9. 3182.40552 _____

Divide. Round the quotient to the nearest tenth.
(Use the long way of dividing or use a calculator.)
(Hint: Divide until that you have 2 decimal places. Then round to the nearest tenth.)

10. $4.7 \div 1.6 =$ _____

11. $18.56 \div 3.55 =$ _____

Divide. Round the quotient to the nearest hundredth.
(Use the long way of dividing or use a calculator.)
(Hint: Divide so that you have 3 decimal places. Then round to the nearest hundredth)

12. $7.25 \div 1.8 =$ _____

13. $85 \div 23 =$ _____

Solve.

14. When Mackey filled up the tank of his car, the meter on the gas pump read 14.73 gallons. The total cost of the gasoline was $18.41. How much does each gallon cost? Round your answer to the nearest cent.
(Hint: How many places do you need so that you can round to the nearest cent?)

_____

Exercises on Your Own

Round each number to the nearest tenth.

1. 3.45 _____

2. 206.081 _____

3. 19.5538 _____

Round to the nearest hundredth.

4. 4.062 _____

5. 400.2876 _____

6. 4.895 _____

Round to the nearest thousandth.

7. 207.9145 _____

8. 45.1234 _____

9. 0.5515 _____

Divide. Round the quotient to the nearest hundredth.
(Use the long way of dividing or use a calculator.)

10. 15.28 ÷ 9.58 = _____

11. 170.5 ÷ 9 = _____

Divide. Round the quotient to the nearest thousandth.
(Use the long way of dividing or use a calculator.)

12. 46 ÷ 27 = _____

13. 8.2 ÷ 7 = _____

Solve.

14. Ruben earned $457.89 last week. He worked 29 hours. How much does he earn each hour? Round the answer to the nearest cent.

_____

15. Jessica drove 235.4 miles last Thursday on a business trip. The trip took 4.7 hours. What was the average speed of the trip? Round your answer to the nearest tenth.

_____

16. At the annual December party, Sheryl's department drank two large bowls of juice, 3.8 liters each. There were 13 people at the party. What was the average amount each person drank? Round your answer to the nearest tenth.

_____

7.8 Fractions to Decimals

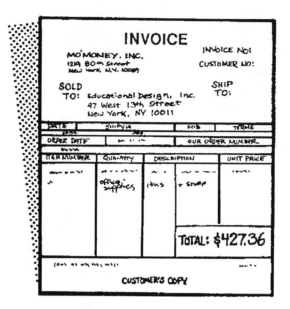

The boss wants José's department to pay $\frac{3}{4}$ of a bill for office supplies, since most of the supplies were used by José's department. The bill was $427.36. How much is José's department being asked to pay?

Solve this problem by multiplying $\frac{3}{4}$ by $427.36.

To make the multiplication easier, change the fraction 3/4 to a decimal:

$\frac{3}{4}$ means 3 divided by 4

$$
\begin{array}{r}
.75 \\
4 \overline{) 3.00} \\
-28 \\
\hline
20 \\
-20 \\
\hline
0
\end{array}
$$

$\frac{3}{4}$ = 0.75

427.36 × 0.75 = **?**

You can do this on a calculator or do it by multiplying out.

427.36 × 0.75 = 320.52

Jose's department will pay $320.52.

Frequently, it is easier to change a fraction to a decimal before you make a computation.

HOW TO *change a fraction to a decimal:*

1. Divide the numerator of the fraction by the denominator.

2. If the fraction is a fraction greater than 1 (sometimes called an *improper* fraction), change it to a mixed number first. Then change the fractional part to a decimal.

EXAMPLE 1

Change $\frac{7}{8}$ to a decimal:

Divide 7 by 8:

$$
\begin{array}{r}
.875 \\
8\,\overline{)7.000} \\
-\,6\,4 \\
\hline
60 \\
-\,56 \\
\hline
40 \\
-\,40 \\
\hline
0
\end{array}
$$

$\frac{7}{8} = 0.875$

You can also find the decimal for $\frac{7}{8}$ by using a calculator.

EXAMPLE 2

Change $\frac{27}{5}$ to a decimal.

Change $\frac{27}{5}$ to a mixed number first:

$$\frac{27}{5} = 5\frac{2}{5}$$

Change the fractional part to a decimal and write a mixed decimal. Either divide the long way or use a calculator.

$$\frac{2}{5} = 0.4$$

So, $5\frac{2}{5} = 5.4$

TABLE OF DECIMAL EQUIVALENTS

It is useful to know the decimal equivalents of several common fractions. You can save time if you memorize the equivalencies shown in the table below.

FRACTION DECIMAL	FRACTION DECIMAL
Halves	**Eighths**
$\frac{1}{2}$ = 0.5	$\frac{1}{8}$ = 0.125
	$\frac{3}{8}$ = 0.375
Fourths	$\frac{5}{8}$ = 0.625
$\frac{1}{4}$ = 0.25	$\frac{7}{8}$ = 0.875
$\frac{3}{4}$ = 0.75	
Fifths	**Tenths**
$\frac{1}{5}$ = 0.2	$\frac{1}{10}$ = 0.1
$\frac{2}{5}$ = 0.4	$\frac{3}{10}$ = 0.3
$\frac{3}{5}$ = 0.6	**Thirds**
$\frac{4}{5}$ = 0.8	$\frac{1}{3}$ = 0.333...*
	$\frac{2}{3}$ = 0.666...*

* These are repeating decimals; the three dots means the numbers continue in the same way, repeating the last number forever.

Exercises with Hints

Which of these are proper fractions (fractions less than 1)?

(Hint: the numerator of a proper fraction is less than the denominator.)

1. $\frac{2}{3}$ _____

2. $\frac{7}{6}$ _____

3. $\frac{7}{9}$ _____

4. $\frac{11}{10}$ _____

5. $\frac{5}{5}$ _____

Are the correct division setups shown for finding a decimal for the fractions? Check yes or no.

(Hint: $\frac{4}{5}$ means the same as 4 divided by 5.)

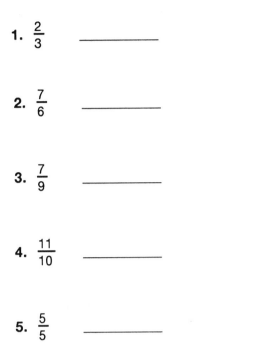

		Yes	No
6. $\frac{4}{5}$	$5\overline{)4}$	____	____
7. $\frac{3}{8}$	$3\overline{)8}$	____	____
8. $\frac{5}{11}$	$11\overline{)5}$	____	____

Find the decimal equivalent for each fraction.

(Hint: You can use the table, or use a calculator, or do the long division.)

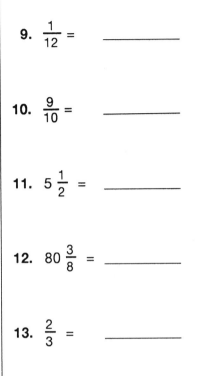

9. $\frac{1}{12}$ = _____

10. $\frac{9}{10}$ = _____

11. $5\frac{1}{2}$ = _____

12. $80\frac{3}{8}$ = _____

13. $\frac{2}{3}$ = _____

Solve.

14. Jack said he paid $23\frac{3}{4}$ for the tools he bought at the lumber yard. Write this amount in dollars and cents.

   (Hint: Use the table to find the fractional equivalent for the decimal.)

   _____

15. Jody worked 14.375 hours last weekend according to the computer printout. Write this amount as a mixed number.

   _____

147

Exercises on Your Own

Put a check mark after all of the following fractions that are fractions greater than 1 (the so-called "improper" fractions).

1. $\frac{5}{3}$ _____

2. $\frac{4}{4}$ _____

3. $\frac{33}{25}$ _____

4. $\frac{5}{7}$ _____

To find the decimal equivalent for these numbers, which number do you divide by (called the divisor)? Write the correct number.

5. $\frac{4}{11}$ _____

6. $\frac{7}{9}$ _____

7. $\frac{2}{15}$ _____

8. $43\frac{3}{16}$ _____

Find the decimal equivalent for each fraction. Use any of the methods you have learned: dividing numerator by denominator, using a calculator, using the table, or dividing by 10, 100, or 1000.

9. $\frac{2}{5}$ _____

10. $\frac{5}{8}$ _____

11. $\frac{6729}{1000}$ _____

12. $\frac{5}{16}$ _____

13. $\frac{7}{25}$ _____

14. $\frac{73}{100}$ _____

15. $54\frac{2}{3}$ _____

Solve.

16. Gary bought 100 shares of a stock in a company that makes medical products. Each share sold for $15 $\frac{5}{8}$. How much is the total amount in dollars and cents?

_____

17. Dolly sells computers. She tells a customer that the special discount on a Baldwin computer is $\frac{2}{5}$ of the regular selling price of the computer. How much is the discount if the regular selling price is $2375?

_____

18. Michael said that his family's new table is $\frac{3}{5}$ as long as their old table. The old table was 2.45 meters long. How long is the new table?

_____

148

Write the decimal point in each quotient.

1. $621.36 ÷ 24 = $2589

2. 57.915 ÷ 45 = 1287

Divide.

3. 787.2 ÷ 8 = _____

4. 838.224 ÷ 12 = _____

5. $214.56 ÷ 24 = _____

6. $55.44 ÷ 6 = _____

Divide.

7. 5 ÷ 8 = _____

8. 2.009 ÷ 5 = _____

9. $18.33 ÷ 12 = _____

10. 15 ÷ 8 = _____

11. $496.38 ÷ 12 = _____

How many places would you move the decimal point to the left when you divide by these numbers?

12. 1000 _____ places

13. 10 _____ places

14. 10,000 _____ places

By what number did we divide the decimal on the left to get the quotient on the right?

	Number Started With	Divided By	Quotient
15.	59.23	_____	0.5923
16.	1298.5	_____	1.2985
17.	0.7	_____	0.0007

Divide.

18. 43.781 ÷1000 = _____

19. 0.45 ÷ 10 = _____

20. 5 ÷ 1000 = _____

Do you have to multiply or divide to find the correct equivalents? (You don't have to work out the problems.)

21. 6592 grams = ____ kilograms
multiply ___   divide ___

22. 239 milliliters = ____ liters
multiply ___   divide ___

23. 87 centimeters = ____ meters
multiply ___   divide ___

24. 14.67 liters = ____ milliliters
multiply ___   divide ___

25. 26.43 millimeters = ___ centimeters
multiply ___   divide ___

Find the missing measures.

26. 6592 grams = _____ kilograms

27. 239 milliliters = _____ liters

28. 87 centimeters = _____ meters

29. 14.67 liters = _____ milliliters

30. 26.43 millimeters = _____ centimeters

Divide.

31. 36.4 ÷ 2.6 = _____

32. 205.4 ÷ 7.9 = _____

33. 212.16 ÷ 13.6 = _____

34. 105.84 ÷ 18.9 = _____

Round each to the nearest tenth.

35. 17.52 _____

36. 105.072 _____

Round to the nearest hundredth.

37. 8.925 _____

38. 1407.083 _____

Round to the nearest thousandth.

39. 0.5828 _____

40. 499.9995 _____

Divide. Round the quotient to the nearest hundredth.
(Use the long way of dividing or use a calculator.)

41. 44.67 ÷ 7.24 = _____

42. 154.85 ÷ 4.87 = _____

Divide. Round the quotient to the nearest thousandth.
(Use the long way of dividing or use a calculator.)

43. 75.8 ÷ 9.4 = _____

44. 894.91 ÷ 7.8 = _____

Which of these are improper fractions (fractions greater than 1)?

45. $\frac{7}{8}$ _____

46. $\frac{4}{5}$ _____

47. $\frac{21}{21}$ _____

Find the decimal equivalent for each fraction. Use any of the methods you have learned: dividing numerator by denominator, calculator, the table, or dividing by 10, 100, or 1000.

48. $\frac{2}{25}$ = _____

49. $\frac{9}{16}$ = _____

50. $4\frac{915}{1000}$ = _____

51. $\frac{3}{5}$ = _____

52. $4\frac{2}{3}$ = _____

53. $8\frac{5}{8}$ = _____

54. $3\frac{4}{100}$ = _____

Solve.

55. Mariana ordered 17 trophies for graduation day ceremonies. The total cost was $318.75. What was the cost of each trophy?

_____

56. Rosa's annual salary is $40,230. She receives a salary check every month. How much is her monthly salary?

_____

57. The eight people in Eric's department shared part of the company's profits last year. They split $4250. If they split the bonus money equally, how much did each person get?

_____

58. Fran has to make a budget for the next 10 months. For travel, she has allotted $3,876. How much is that going to be for each month?

_____

59. The length of Carl's backyard is 16.87 meters. He divided the length into 10 equal parts as part of his plan to build a vegetable garden. How long is each part?

_____

60. Profits of the Design Unique Company have grown 1000 times over the past 7 years. Profits this year are $346,892. How much profit did the company make the first year?

_____

61. Lucy said that she did not understand her weight when she was told she weighed 48,500 grams. Write Lucy's weight in kilograms.

_____

62. Derek measured the amount of water he used in an experiment very carefully. He measured the volume of water as 2.56 liters. Write the amount of water in milliliters.

_____

63. The diameter of a computer disk is 89 millimeters. Write this length in centimeters.

_____

64. Margo weighed several packages together and found that they weighed 64.8 pounds. If each package weighs 5.4 pounds, how many packages did Margo weigh?

_____

65. Jim received credit for 5.4 days of making telephone sales calls. The total amount that he brought in was $996.30. What was the average amount he brought in per day?

_____

66. Having worked 25.9 hours, Otis earned $387.50. How much does he earn each hour? Round the answer to the nearest cent.

_____

67. Leonia read her telephone bill very carefully. It showed that she made 19 phone calls totaling $78.75. What was the average cost of each phone call? (Round the answer to the nearest cent.)

_____

68. Leroy spoke for $4\frac{2}{5}$ hours. Write this mixed number as a decimal.

_____

69. Teresa sold 200 shares of Golden Ray Company for $42\frac{3}{8}$. Write this mixed number as a decimal.

_____

70. The length of a conference table was 3.25 meters. Write this decimal as a mixed number.

_____

71. The distance from Jed's home to the beach is 4.125 miles. Write this decimal number as a mixed number.

_____

10.95   8-06-01